This is a very good job reconciling the weird stories of Mexico City and New Orleans, which created an unbelievable Lee Harvey Oswald who was simply too many characters in one person. And it explains better than any other book how the events of November were played out with two Oswalds. As a result, almost all of the inconsistencies are reconciled. Fascinating.

Paul Schulte

Great book, well written, a hard-to-put-down read.

Bjørk

Recommend to all. Excellent logic and research. One of the best works on the JFK murder I have read.

Joseph A. Cammalleri

I couldn't stop reading until I had finished the last page.

Reading Ghost

An incredible amount of research, documentation, and brilliant analysis. The book was infectious, and I could hardly wait to read the next page.

MW

An amazing narrative – appears to be very well researched.

David H. Koehler

Also by George Schwimmer PhD

The Search For David
Adventures In Consciousness
DAVID: leaves from the journal of a soul (ed.)
Muzungu Wendy (ed.)
MU: The First Great Civilization
Healing Secrets of the Shamans of Mu
Robert Monroe's Altered States
My Past Lives And Life Plan
A. R. MARTIN: Pioneer In Past Life Regression
The Littlest Soul
Hamlet Dead (a play)
Cayce (a play)

DOPPELGÄNGER

THE LEGEND OF LEE HARVEY OSWALD

GEORGE SCHWIMMER PhD

PHOENIX 11 PRODUCTIONS
Santa Fe, New Mexico

Phoenix 11 Productions
Santa Fe, New Mexico

Copyright © 2016 by George Schwimmer PhD

All rights reserved, including the right to reproduce this work or portions thereof in any form whatsoever without permission in writing from the author, except for brief passages in connection with a review. To contact the author: www.GeorgeSchwimmer.com.

First trade paperback edition April, 2016

Book and cover design by George Schwimmer PhD

Manufactured in the United States of America

Publisher's Cataloging-In-Publication Data

Schwimmer, George.
 Doppelgänger: the legend of Lee Harvey Oswald / George Schwimmer PhD.
 First paper edition. | Santa Fe, New Mexico: Phoenix 11 Productions, 2016.
 Includes bibliographical references.
 ISBN: 978-1-5303-6498-5 (paper)
 ASIN: B00VB507GA (Kindle ebook)
 LCSH: Oswald, Lee Harvey. | Kennedy, John F. (John Fitzgerald), 1917-1963--Assassination. | Assassins--United States. | Conspiracies—United States--History--20th century.
 LCC E842.9 .S39 2016 | DDC 364.152/4--dc23

Contents

Harvey's Introduction	*1*
Two Oswalds	*5*
The Mothers	*11*
Doppelgänger Marines	*17*
Harvey & Hungary	*25*
Murrets & Oswalds	*31*
The Legend Begins	*39*
Texas	*45*
New Orleans	*51*
'Oswalds' Everywhere	*71*
Back To Dallas	*81*
Friday, November 22, 1963	*97*
Ambush	*111*
TSBD Entryway – 12:31	*119*
Escape & The Witnesses	*137*
To And From 1026	*169*

Shooting Of J. D. Tippit	*187*
The Rifle(s)	*205*
Texas Theatre – Lies & Liars	*211*
The Patsy & "A. J. Hidell"	*243*
Booked & Questioned	*255*
Wesley Frazier Again	*259*
Arraigned	*265*
Backyard Photo	*269*
Execution & Funeral	*283*
Aftermath	*287*
Afterword	*297*
What Happened To:	*307*
Author's Note	*311*
Acknowledgment	*313*
Sources	*315*
Author	*323*

doppelgänger: an apparition or physical double of a living person

Harvey's Introduction

> *When you have eliminated the impossible, whatever remains, however improbable, must be the truth.*
>
> *Sherlock Holmes*
> Arthur Conan Doyle

Although I'm long dead, I know there are people left who still hate me. And if I'd done what I was accused of, I'd accept what I deserved. But actually I was a loyal American serving my country. I killed no one. I liked and respected John Kennedy, believed he was a man of peace. If you think you know who I was, I've got just two words for you: you don't. Because, in spite of being known as "Lee Harvey Oswald," that wasn't me – though there *was* a real Lee Harvey Oswald, who went by the name Lee. I was his doppelgänger, 'Harvey.' We both were CIA agents.

Most accounts of me are not only badly-drawn caricatures, but also include facts from the life of the real Lee Oswald. See, if you work under deep cover for an intelligence service, almost no one can recognize who you are, because you wear a mask – it's called a 'legend,' a fictitious portrait. And when push comes to shove, your handlers will always deny knowing you, and your records will be hidden, falsified and trashed – if they ever existed.

But for now I'd like you to put aside the lies you've been told about me, so that I can give you my real story: how I became a patsy – a fall-guy – for the most vicious plot ever in American politics, which not only murdered JFK and perverted American history but created a great wound in America's soul that's festering even now. I wasn't "a lone nut" who shot JFK – it was a huge high-level conspiracy that killed John F. Kennedy and then covered it all up. I wasn't part of it.

We can start with who wanted President Kennedy dead: Cuban exiles who hated him for refusing air cover for the Bay of Pigs invasion, the Central Intelligence Agency (CIA) which JFK said he'd splinter into a thousand pieces, the Mafia dons who despised the Kennedy brothers and wanted to recover their gambling casinos in Cuba, and big Texas oil men who wanted JFK out of the White House and Lyndon Johnson in. There also were some military men who lusted for war against Cuba, Vietnam and even Russia, J. Edgar Hoover who feared and hated the Kennedys, the rulers of the Federal Reserve Bank, and of course Lyndon

Johnson himself, a ruthless man who loathed the Kennedys and was obsessed with becoming president. Most were furious with JFK's peace overtures to Khrushchev to end the Cold War, considering Kennedy a traitor.

Let's see which of these had their fingers in *my* pie.

Doppelgänger: The Legend Of Lee Harvey Oswald

Two Oswalds

The first faint thread of the 'Oswald' saga showed up when Lee Oswald was eight and living in New Orleans. Lee's father had died two months before Lee's birth on October 18, 1939, and eventually his mother, Marguerite, couldn't make ends meet. So, in '42 his two older brothers, John Pic, 10, and Robert Oswald, 8, were sent to a children's home, while young Lee was cared for during the next year by his mother's sister Lillian and her husband, Charles "Dutz" Murret, a bookie with close ties to crime boss Carlos Marcello.

Around '47, Dutz met a Dallas mob associate of Marcello, Jack Ruby (Jacob "Sparky" Rubenstein), a Chicago hood who moved permanently to Dallas in '47 and opened two nightclubs there. In '47 Ruby was a hired informant of Congressman Richard M. Nixon, having been recommended to Nixon by Congressman Lyndon B. Johnson, Ruby being one of "Lyndon's boys." In the late '50s Ruby ran guns to Cuba by boat.

Dutz took Marguerite Oswald and Lee to some parties given by Carlos Marcello, where Lee and Jack Ruby might have crossed paths. It's ironic that the man who may have patted the real Lee Harvey Oswald on his head at a New Orleans party when Lee was a kid, years later shot me to death in Dallas.

In August, 1952, when Lee was twelve and I was eleven, he and his mother – then living in Fort Worth, Texas – suddenly moved to New York City, where I lived. That's when I – by then also known as Lee Harvey Oswald – first surfaced. At that time I was only about 4'6" tall and thin (70-75 pounds), while Lee was 5'4", 114 pounds, and was described as "the tallest, the dominant school kid" in his class the previous semester. I was now in seventh grade, Lee was in eighth grade. My 'cousin' Marilyn Murret, Dutz's daughter, later testified to the *Warren Commission* (WC), "Lee was extremely quiet." She was talking about *me, Harvey* – Lee was the opposite of quiet.

His Uncle Dutz told the WC, "[Lee] was a loud kid; he was always raising his voice when he wanted something from his mother." Myrtle Evans, a New Orleans friend of Marguerite, said that when Lee wanted supper "he would scream like a bull. He would holler, 'Maw, where's my supper?' Lee was about thirteen then and had a loud voice." Myrtle's husband, Julian, felt Lee "was arrogant, and no one liked him," thought that Lee was "a psycho" and "very loud and insolent." Three classmates, girls, could only remember Lee as "always getting into fights."

Once in New York, Lee and his mother moved in with his brother John Pic and John's wife Margaret (Margy). John had been stationed at Coast Guard Base St. George, Staten Island, N.Y. from June, 1951 until January, 1952, and then from April, 1952 until February, 1953 he was stationed at Ellis Island (where European immigrants disembarked when arriving in the U.S.), with the intelligence unit of the Coast Guard, Port Security Unit (PSU), which was "tasked with keeping the ports clear of subversives. They did this in partnership with the FBI, ONI [Office of Naval Intelligence] and a network of informants," researcher Greg Parker has written.

Not yet thirteen, Lee continued his explosive behavior. John later testified, "If Lee decided to do something, regardless of what my mother said, he did it. She had no authority whatsoever with him. He had no respect for her at all." John claimed that during an argument over which TV show to watch, Lee pulled a pocket knife on Margy and threatened her, then struck his mother. As a result, Margy asked them to move out, and they went to live in the Bronx, John said. No way to corroborate the knife incident. There were, however, teachers' notes that Lee had a quick temper, lost control often, and got into fights.

I, Harvey, played hooky from school during the next eighteen months, rode the subways, went to museums and read a lot. A probation officer described me as *"a small boy*, a bright boy, a likeable one, but *extremely guarded when discussing certain areas of his life."*

I finally was sent to Youth House in April, 1953, where all of the staff commented on my "frail appearance." A psychiatrist said I was "a slender boy with a pale, haunted face…how slight he seemed for his thirteen years." I was only twelve – I'd been told to use Lee's birth date. "He had an underfed look reminiscent of starved children…in concentration camps." The psychiatrist wrote in his report that I had a "superior mental endowment" but also that I was a "disturbed youngster, who suffers emotional isolation and deprivation, lack of affection, and rejection by a self-involved mother."

Another psychiatrist – who knew me as "Harvey" – said I "was very quiet and introverted." I told him about my mother's five marriages and that all but one of my stepfathers had been cruel to me. I spoke of my brothers, who often provoked me to the point of "blind rage." One would hold my head at arm's length and laugh as I flailed the air trying to hit him, I said. I never went to school, but a brother once went to class in my place.

People may think those odd family accounts of mine were just fantasies of a disturbed boy, but I wasn't just a little dreamy kid by then – I was almost thirteen, *and I actually was talking about my real birth family.* Can you see why I was glad to leave that family and perform a service for my new country? Oh, yes, I was a Hungarian immigrant, and you can assume my birth mother was no longer living.

Doppelgänger: The Legend Of Lee Harvey Oswald

The Mothers

Then who was the "self-involved mother" that the psychiatrist mentioned? Her real identity still isn't known – she always said she was "Marguerite Oswald." However, multiple witnesses who knew Marguerite Claverie Oswald describe *two very different* 'Marguerites.' People who had known the real Marguerite in the mid to late '50s couldn't in 1963 recognize pictures of my 'mother' as the same person. Two of these people, Myrtle and Julian Evans, had known the real Marguerite *for thirty years*!

Julian testified before the WC, first about the *real* Marguerite, "A fine woman...intelligent, very soft spoken – a beautiful woman, with black hair streaked with a little gray.... She used to be a fashion plate...." And then, the *bogus* Marguerite, "When you saw her on television [now] ...she really looked awful...looked like a charwoman.... You wouldn't have recognized her if they hadn't told you who she was; she looked that different." Told Marguerite was 57, Julian said, "That's right; she's the same age as my wife, but [this Marguerite] looks about 70 now."

1943   1945   1947   1957

The first Marguerite (above), born in 1907, was tall (about 5'7"), slim and trim, attractive, smartly-dressed, intelligent, with a pleasant personality – most of her photographs show her smiling. She was known to work in sales of apparel (far right photo).

'Aunt' Lillian testified to the WC that "[Marguerite was] a very beautiful girl, and she doesn't look today at all like she used to, you know. You wouldn't recognize her.... I don't think that she was resentful of anybody.... She was very entertaining. She could sing very well...had a good voice...and she learned to play by ear on the piano, so we really had a lot of fun." This Marguerite was *Lee's* mother.

The second 'Marguerite' was short (less than 5'1"), squat, fat, unattractive, poorly dressed, with a very unpleasant personality – most of her photos show her unsmiling (next page). The real Marguerite Oswald was fifty-six years old when I died. Does the 'Marguerite'

The Mothers

1954   1962   1963   1964

above look about fifty-six (two photos on the right) or forty seven (in the far left photo)? A young friend I once had in New Orleans, Palmer McBride, in 1963 described my 'mother' *in 1957* as being "short and fat." He identified the 1954 picture above as my 'mother.' Palmer McBride was never interviewed by the WC.

This woman was known to work as a practical nurse. She also was employed once as a cashier at a New Orleans shoe store, in 1955. She was described as unfriendly, a constant complainer who never smiled. Being the cashier, her boss required her to be bonded. He gave her the forms to fill out, but she never completed them, nor would she give a straight answer why she didn't, so she was fired – and went on to work as a barmaid! This 'Marguerite' was *my* 'mother.'

A reporter who drove her to the police station just hours after JFK's assassination later wrote, "She was a very peculiar person and she immediately began to talk about how nobody would feel sorry for her – they'd feel sympathy for [Lee's] wife and give her money. She was completely obsessed with money. She expressed no remorse about the president being killed." Another reporter described her as "a thoroughly disagreeable piece of work – manipulative, abrasive, and mercenary to a fault." After November, 1963, neither her 'sons' Robert and John, nor my wife Marina, ever saw her or spoke with her again.

At any rate, in the summer of '53 I and my 'mother' went to Stanley, North Dakota, where I introduced myself to some boys as "Harvey" from New York City. In the fall I and my 'mother' moved to a sleazy part of New Orleans' French Quarter, where Lee had been born, and I enrolled in Beauregard Junior High School, while Lee attended PS 44 in New York City, where, the WC later reported, "Lee was disruptive in class...[and] became a disciplinary problem." Lee and his mother came back to New Orleans in '54.

In January, 1954, my eighth grade home room teacher at Beauregard was Myra DaRouse, who later told researcher John Armstrong that I was "a little fellow, scrawny, skinny and quiet. He came to the middle of my chest – about 4 foot 6 inches tall.... The first day he came into my home room he handed me his file. When I read his name was Lee Harvey Oswald, I said to him, 'How do you want to be called,' and he told me to call him 'Harvey.' So, I called him 'Harvey.' I knew him only as 'Harvey.'"

Shown the picture below, taken at the Bronx Zoo in 1953, Myra told John Armstrong, "That's [Harvey], just like I remember him." When Lee's brother John appeared before the WC and was shown this picture, he said, "Sir, from that photo I could not recognize that is Lee Harvey Oswald." Lee's brother Robert testified that he had taken the photograph and that the figure in it was his brother Lee. So, the teacher who saw me for a semester said it was 'Harvey,' one brother said it was Lee, the other brother said it definitely wasn't Lee. Someone was lying.

Doppelgänger: The Legend Of Lee Harvey Oswald

Doppelgänger Marines

David Ferrie (left) and Lee Oswald (right) at a CAP outing.

During the spring of '55 Lee joined a New Orleans chapter of the Civil Air Patrol (CAP) led by David Ferrie, whose dream of becoming a Catholic priest was derailed by his taste for teenage boys, which also cost him his commercial airline pilot's job. Ferrie became deeply involved with anti-Castro elements, with the FBI and the CIA, with Carlos Marcello, and with running guns to Cuba by air, just as Jack Ruby had run guns by sea.

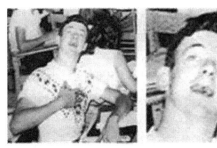

Late 1954 – Lee, clowning in school. An upper front tooth is missing. Also notice his wide neck, long and thick arms, and the almost parallel sides of his head.

Lee's brother Robert had joined the Marines in '52, so in October '55, when he was sixteen, Lee tried to lie his way into the Marine Corps. Didn't succeed. But in '56 he did. Eventually he was sent to the Atsugi Naval Air Base in Japan, home of the U-2 spy plane. While there, the Office of Naval Intelligence (ONI) and the CIA used him to start setting up my 'legend' of being 'a bad boy.' This was part of "The Oswald Project," funds for which were disbursed by the CIA in Japan.

In order to build the 'legend' that would give *me*, the 'legend' Lee Harvey Oswald, a background for a covert assignment to Russia, Lee went to the expensive Tokyo nightclub Queen Bee, which was frequented by Russian operatives, where he passed along fake information to a Russian KGB agent and became involved with an attractive

Eurasian girl who asked him about U-2 flights. He got into a phony fist fight off-base with his sergeant, 'accidentally' shot himself with a .22 caliber derringer, was court-martialed twice and supposedly spent 45 days in the brig. Pictures of Lee are below.

The 1958 photo was taken by Robert Oswald when Lee was on leave from the Marines – check the receding hairline and wide neck. Notice: there are no cleft chins. In the 1959 passport photo, Lee's hairline was touched up by the CIA. That picture seems to be a composite of Lee and me, Harvey.

The Lee Harvey Oswald at Atsugi was 5'11", a husky 165 pounds, hazel eyes, left-handed, had almost black receding hair like a widow's peak, no hair part, no cleft chin, a front tooth knocked out, his tonsils removed, a mastoidectomy scar behind his left ear, a vaccination scar, a tattoo and two gunshot scars on his left arm, an I.Q. of 103, was nicknamed "Ozzie," would fight anyone who called him "Harvey" or "Harv." Occasionally, he'd talk about his family.

He was not interested in politics, did not subscribe to Russian newspapers, never studied, read, or spoke Russian in barracks. He was a good shot with a rifle, would get drunk, and got into fights. He learned to speak fluent Spanish. After he left the Marines, he worked as an anti-Castro ONI/CIA operative in New Orleans, Florida, Havana and Dallas. He could drive a car, had a Texas driver's license, and got a haircut every two weeks – cropped short, *squared in the back*, right up to November 22, 1963.

I also joined the Marines in '56 and was brought into the false defector program of the ONI. I was a mediocre shot with a rifle (my Marine buddies ridiculed me for my shooting, and the Russkies later reported I was a terrible shot with a shotgun), never drank, didn't fight, didn't drive, had no driver's license, never talked about my family.

1956 – Me, Harvey, described as "scrawny" by a teacher, shortly before I joined the Marine Corps.

I grew to 5'9", 135 pounds, blue-gray eyes, right-handed, a pointed and cleft chin, medium brown hair, no widow's peak – parted on the left side, never close-cropped or squared, rarely got a haircut, had an I.Q. of 118 and was *never* called "Ozzie." At death I had my tonsils, no tooth missing, no mastoidectomy scar, no vaccination scar, no tattoo and no gunshot scars on my left arm – see my autopsy report.

I spoke fluent, almost unaccented, Russian, *no* Spanish. I read Russian newspapers, preached Marxist communism in my barracks, and also spun a second thread: admiring the Castro-led Cuban revolution – even voicing my desire to join Castro's revolutionary army. These two threads were twisted together to form my 'legend' until I died, and for years afterwards.

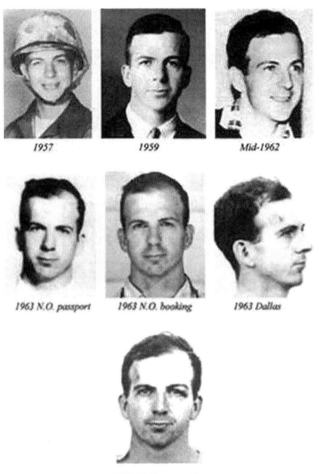

1963 Dallas booking

Pictures of me, Harvey. Note that there's no missing front tooth. The 1959 (center) and 1963 (left) photos may be composites - half my face, half Lee's.

Keep in mind, though, that when I went into the Marine Corps I was just 16-17 years old and became an undercover operative who said and did what he was told in order to create and maintain his 'legend.' So you can't accept at face value *anything* I said, wrote or did from then on, since it was mostly the 'legend' talking and acting, not me. In fact, once I joined the Marines I wasn't *me* any more – I *was* the 'legend' 'Lee Harvey Oswald' until I died. But I was proud to be in the Marines, proud of the intelligence work I was doing – remember, I was just an immigrant kid with limited education. This was a big deal for me.

Late in '57 I received intensive training in spycraft at the CIA's Camp Peary, and when Lee returned to the U. S. in December, 1958, I took his place, while Lee went to the Army Language School by Monterey Bay to learn to speak Spanish. This is when fellow Marines noticed my interest in all things Russian. Toward the end of my Marine service I was stationed in Southern California, where the ONI taught me interrogation resistance techniques. Those came in handy in Moscow – and when the Dallas police later questioned me. During my last two weeks in the Marines I was constantly at my base's Criminal Investigative Division, being briefed on my overseas mission.

As my story continues to unfold, keep your eyes on 'my' photographs and see if you think they all are of the same man. For a start, take a look at the following four pictures of 'me' on the next page:

Doppelgänger: The Legend Of Lee Harvey Oswald

Marines *Marines*

Compare the widths of the two necks.

Passport photo. *Booking photo.*

Notice the ear at left is larger and set higher on the head. And the neck at left is wider. Eye at right is deep-set.

Harvey & Hungary

Rewind a few years. I was chosen to become an intelligence operative very early on, since my life and Lee's began to converge in '52. How could this happen, and who made it happen?

I was silenced before I could tell what I knew, but there are clues. First, Russian is a very difficult language to master. How could I have learned to speak *fluent* Russian in the Marines? No one learns to speak fluent Russian from a book, nor to easily read Cyrillic script (БГДЂГЖ). Yet my wife Marina commented that when she met me she thought I was a native Russian, speaking with just a slight Baltic accent, and Peter Paul Gregory, a Dallas Russian émigré, three years later thought it was a Polish accent.

Speaking of accents, I had a New York accent. 'Cousin' Marilyn – eleven years older than Lee – testified that when 'Lee' was a schoolboy, other students in New Orleans "didn't like him because of his [Northern] accent, and because he sat next to Negroes [on a streetcar]." She wasn't speaking about Lee, of course, but me. She also said, of my 1963 time in New Orleans, "It seems that he was from the North.... His accent was very good. I mean he pronounced every syllable, and the word endings were always pronounced – and he was just very quiet." That was me. A classmate in the spring of 1954, Ed Collier, recalled, "We called him Yank because he had a Yankee accent."

Jean Mohrenschildt – a later family friend – said she had been amazed by my English speech – that I spoke very precisely and deliberately, rarely using slang. She wondered where a boy who had been brought up in the South had learned to speak like that. Listen to recordings of my voice and see if you can detect a Southern drawl. My Marine friend Kerry Thornley, from New Orleans, noticed I spoke with no southern dialect – if anything, that I had a New York accent.

After my death, my recorded speech was analyzed by three university language specialists, who weren't told to whose voice they were listening. All agreed that English was not the native birth language of the man speaking – that his English seemed to have been acquired later in life.

Then, after Dallas Police Officer J. D. Tippit's murder, an anonymous woman with a foreign accent phoned one of

Tippit's distant relatives in Westport, Connecticut and said that she personally knew my real father and uncle, who were Hungarian immigrants and active communists, unemployed, living in Manhattan, at *East 77th Street and 2nd Avenue [Yorkville]*. Yorkville was a haven for refugees from communist regimes in the 1950s.

The woman said she feared for her life if anyone found out she'd made the call. She even mentioned a Hungarian name – Emil Kardos (the FBI report spelled it "Emile"). The 1940 Census listed an Emil Kardos at *320 E. 80th Street (near 2nd Avenue)*, Manhattan – birthplace Hungary, non-citizen, 66, unemployed, widower, who had a 34-year-old son with the same name, also born in Hungary, living with him – three blocks from where my father was said to live in 1963. Younger Emil would have been 57 years old in 1963, and could have been a 'communist' *agent provocateur* for the FBI in the late 1940s and 1950s.

A second name she mentioned was Louis Weinstock, who was then the Hungarian-born leader of the Communist Party USA, 60 years old in 1963, and who in 1950 was tried in New York City for communist related activities but was acquitted. In December of 1962, I wrote to Weinstock, who was then business manager of *The Worker*.

In Hungary, Russian is an oft-spoken second language. Professor Vladimir Petrov, head of the Slavic Language Department of Yale University, studied a handwritten letter I'd sent from Russia to U.S Senator John Tower of Texas in 1962. Petrov wrote to Sen. Tower, "The person who wrote the letter was a native-speaking Russian with an imperfect knowledge of the English language."

In that letter I wrote, "My name is Lee Harvey Oswald, 22, of Fort Worth up till October 1959, when I came to the Soviet Union for a residenaul [sic] stay. I took a residenual [sic] document for a non-Soviet person living for a time in the USSR.... I beseech you, Senator Tower, to rise [sic] the question of holding by the Soviet Union of a citizen of the U.S., against his will and expressed desires!!" Don't need a language professor to see that's not something a good old boy raised in New Orleans and Fort Worth would write. And on my handwritten visa application to leave Russia, for my place of birth I put down "New Orleans, Texas." By the way, my spelling was always poor. People have written that I may have been dyslexic.

Two more odd facts: first, in 1951 my 'brother' John Pic married Margaret Fuhrman, whose parents had been *born in Hungary* and whose widowed mother lived at *325*

East 92nd Street (near 2nd Avenue), Yorkville (part of which area – East 79th Street to East 83rd Street, and 3rd Avenue to the East River, Manhattan – was known as "Little Hungary").

So, how did John (then in the Coast Guard PSU intelligence unit) happen to meet his wife Margy – and did *John and Margy* have anything to do with the CIA finding me when I was ten or eleven? Had John been assigned to work with the PSU at Ellis Island to look for a Russian-speaking boy who resembled his younger brother Lee? Wasn't it a wonderful coincidence that I surfaced in New York City at the same time as John was stationed on Ellis Island and living in Manhattan?

Second, I was issued a passport on September 10, 1959, which was stamped with: "This passport is not valid for travel in Hungary," and no one could ever say why.

Doppelgänger: The Legend Of Lee Harvey Oswald

Murrets & Oswalds

Remember, Lee's uncle Dutz was connected with the Louisiana Mob, which was anti-Castro and worked with the CIA. Dutz's daughter Marilyn Murret was a world-traveling schoolteacher who was a CIA agent. What Marilyn eventually said about 'Lee Harvey Oswald' makes it clear she knew Lee *and* me, Harvey, both as pre-teens and as young men.

Years later 'Aunt' Lillian testified that when Lee was sixteen "he met someone in this branch of the service who had taken a liking to him, and he used to go over there and converse with him about different things in the service and so forth. I don't know who he was or what they talked about." A sixteen-year-old boy who *just* happened to meet a military "someone." A military *intelligence* "someone" is more likely.

Returning to accents, 'brother' Robert testified that when his family moved to Dallas in 1944, he "had something of a southern drawl....I recall having a little difficulty in school to make myself clearly understood." If Robert had a Southern drawl, Lee must have had one too. I didn't, of course.

Incidentally, the last time I was with 'brother' John Pic was at a 1962 Fort Worth Thanksgiving 'family' get-together, to which the bogus 'Marguerite' – also living in Forth Worth then – was *not* invited, probably because John would have seen that she was *not* his mother. John had last been visited by the *real* Marguerite in 1957. John hadn't seen his brother Lee for ten years and later commented that he was *shocked* by how *different* his 'brother' looked.

John testified to the WC, "[Lee] was much thinner than I had remembered him. He didn't have as much hair. His face features were somewhat different; his eyes were set back.... *His face was rounder.* Marilyn [who had met Lee, and later John, in Japan] had described him to me as having a bull neck.... I looked for this, but I didn't notice this at all." Of course not – John wasn't looking at Lee, but at me, Harvey. When I put my current address in John's address book, I wrote my name as "Harvey." John didn't ask why.

When the WC attorney showed John two photographs of me when I was young – one the Bronx Zoo picture – John said *he could not recognize* either of them *as his brother Lee*. Handed another photograph of "Lee Harvey Oswald" wearing a Marine helmet (p. 24), John responded, "I would never guess that that would be Lee." He also said that he did not recognize *as his brother Lee* the picture of *me* handing out leaflets in New Orleans in '63. This was *only eighteen months after he'd met me* in Fort Worth for the 'family' Thanksgiving gathering in '62.

Of course, John *didn't* say he did not recognize *the person* in the photo. He just said it wasn't *Lee*, which it wasn't, and the WC didn't ask him if he knew who *the person* in the photo was. John had sworn to tell *nothing but the truth* – and, in fact, he never lied – but had failed to tell *the whole truth*. Clever 'brother' John – he knew how he needed to play the game. And why wasn't John *shocked* when he saw photographs of the bogus Marguerite?

And let's not forget about Lee's mother, the *real* Marguerite, who hovered in the background of the 'Oswald legend,' remembering that her sister's husband was associated with Carlos Marcello, that Marcello was associated with the CIA, that Marguerite went to parties at Marcello's house, and that at one time she dated Marcello's chauffeur/bodyguard. Even putting aside Marguerite's tangled whereabouts, employments and often odd finances, she had to have been consciously involved in the creation of the 'Oswald' 'legend,' if only by her trip to New York City. That trip was crucial to begin merging the lives of the two Lee Harvey Oswalds. That's when I came into the picture, so Marguerite and Lee were needed in New York.

And whatever happened to this Marguerite after 1959? There is a clue: Lillian Murret testified to the WC in '64 that when 'Lee' defected to Russia in '59, "We didn't hear any more from [Marguerite].... When she left here, she said she was going to get lost.... She said nobody was going to know where she was going.... I don't know why, so then I didn't hear from her any more."

Of course, a lot *was heard* from '59 to '64 from the *bogus* 'Marguerite Oswald.' Why didn't 'Aunt' Lillian mention something about any of that? And between September, 1959 (when Lillian last saw her sister) and November, 1963 Marguerite changed so much, Lillian had testified, that "You wouldn't recognize her." Really? Couldn't recognize your own *sister*? Four years later? And she suddenly got fat in four years after being trim all her life – *and shrank six inches*?

And Lillian didn't try to contact her 'sister' after Marguerite's son 'Lee' was shot to death? The little boy who'd lived in Lillian's home for a year? But, of course, Lillian wasn't *that* 'Marguerite's' sister – had never seen or talked to *that* woman, had never taken care of *that* 'Lee' as a little boy. But – jumping ahead – she *had* let *that* 'Lee,' me, stay in her home for five days when I came to New Orleans in April 1963.

John Pic once commented that Robert Oswald knew considerably more than he was saying, was withholding information, and, based on subsequent events, it's obvious Robert knew a great deal, which he didn't reveal, and said and wrote things about me that either never happened or happened to Lee. It's more than possible, since Robert had been in the Marines, that – like me and Lee – he also had been recruited by the ONI and CIA, which would explain a lot that seems inexplicable about Robert Oswald, including that he had lived with me and the bogus 'Marguerite' in 1956. Keep in mind that Robert's cousin, Marilyn, worked for the CIA, and things begin to fall into place.

John, Marilyn, Lillian, Dutz, and the real Marguerite also knew more than they ever said. At a minimum, none of them ever revealed that I and my 'mother' were fakes, substitutions. But they all had to know. And they all must have been scared out of their minds after the assassination, because they all were accessories – before and after the fact – to the murder of JFK, and were obstructing justice. Certainly, they all realized that if they talked, either the CIA or the Mob would kill them – in some very unpleasant way – consequently none of them ever revealed anything, at least not deliberately. They did inadvertently. And Marilyn seems to have consciously slipped in a couple of things for the historical record.

So, what seems to be here is a nest of CIA operatives and enablers. Let's put it all together:

Carlos Marcello. Crime boss of Louisiana, who worked closely with the CIA and helped finance anti-Castro exiles in their bid to retake Cuba. Carlos later claimed he had ordered the 'hit' on JFK.

"Dutz" Murret. A bookie and close associate of Carlos.

Lillian Claverie Murret. His wife, who opened her home to me, Harvey, in 1963, so both she and Dutz had to know I wasn't Lee.

Marilyn Murret. Lillian and Dutz's daughter, a CIA contract agent for many years. May have been partly responsible for her cousins being recruited by the CIA. While in Japan in the late '50s, helped to "facilitate" 'Oswald's' trip to Russia, a CIA source once told a reporter. Knew me from 1953 on, helped to bail me out of jail in the summer of 1963. Her 1977 House *Select Committee on Assassinations* (HSCA) testimony was classified and has never been released.

Marguerite Claverie Oswald. Lillian's sister, who attended parties at Marcello's house and dated two of Carlos' men. Helped to create the "Oswald Legend." Disappeared after the 'defection' of 'Lee Harvey Oswald' in 1959.

John Pic. Marguerite's first son. Joined the Coast Guard in 1950, was attached in 1952 to the Coast Guard PSU intelligence unit, which worked in partnership with the FBI and ONI. He may have had some role in my being recruited by the CIA when I was ten or eleven.

Robert Oswald. Marguerite's second son. Joined the Marines, may have been recruited by the ONI and CIA, and for fifty years has acted the role of 'Lee Harvey Oswald's brother' and 'son' of the bogus 'Marguerite Oswald.'

LEE Harvey Oswald. Recruited by the ONI and CIA, worked for the CIA, helped to set up the 'legend' of 'Lee Harvey Oswald,' probably helped to impersonate and incriminate me.

Plus David Ferrie, who was an associate of Carlos

Marcello, worked with the CIA for years and knew both LEE Oswald and me, HARVEY.

And let's not forget Jack Ruby, lifelong member of the Mob, associated with Carlos Marcello and the CIA, FBI informant, and, as we'll see, associated later with LEE "Ozzie" Oswald.

Now, recall that John Pic lived in New York City in 1952, as did *both* Marguerite Oswalds and *both* Lee Harvey Oswalds, and you've got something to think about.

The Legend Begins

Once out of the Marines, I headed for Russia. My 'mother' later said: "Lee decided all in a minute to go...as if he'd received an order. How could he, in the two days he stayed with me after leaving the military, have arranged so quickly to get a passport, a Soviet visa and passage to Russia?" Yes, indeed, how *did* I manage all that?

And where did the money come from – since I had only $203 in my bank account, my separation pay was $219.20, my boat fare was $220, I gave $100 to my 'mother,' and I reported that I had $700 cash when I arrived in England? So, I must have had at least $1,050, which in 2016 dollars equals $8,600. And how did I get a passport *in six days?*

In any case, my departure for Russia on September 20, 1959 was when I publicly took on the identity of 'Lee Harvey Oswald,' and when my 'mother' publicly took on the identity of 'Marguerite Oswald.' That's when the 'legend' of 'Lee Harvey Oswald' took off and flew for the next fifty months. And the real Marguerite Claverie Oswald disappeared forever. And her son Lee Oswald slipped further into the smoke and mirrors world of the CIA, from which he never emerged.

Should touch on how two CIA agents came to share the same identity. The idea must have originated from Allen Dulles, who was named Deputy Director of Central Intelligence in 1950 and who had thought about using twins in intelligence work. He probably passed this concept on to James Jesus Angleton, who Dulles appointed Director of Counterintelligence, which put Angleton in charge of the Soviet desk, 'running' the false defector program in Russia. That's how all the key connections were made, and that's how I came to be 'run' in Russia by the CIA and wound up being falsely 'run' – continuing to use my covert identity – in the U.S. by a CIA renegade.

My sojourn to the land of the Red Bear was pretty tame. I made a big show of defecting at the American Embassy in Moscow, since I'd been told by my trainers that the embassy was completely bugged by the Soviet security service, the MVD, and that if I made a scene it'd be heard by the Russkies. So I created a racket to bolster my credibility, but I never signed the papers renouncing U.S. citizenship – and I left my passport at the Embassy.

The Legend Begins

The Soviets finally let me stay but – suspecting that I was a CIA agent – sent me to Minsk, which put a crimp in my mission. I worked in a Minsk factory that made radios and TVs, and I was monitored by everyone I knew, including the women I dated. Then there was my marriage to Marina Prussakova, only six weeks after we met. Her uncle was a colonel in the MVD, the Russian Ministry of Internal Affairs, and she wanted to go to the U.S. Took us a year to get an exit permit approved, during which time my first daughter, June, was born.

In the U.S., Lee Oswald was working in the shadows as a CIA contract agent in New Orleans and Miami. Jim Marrs wrote that some people who later met Lee in New Orleans described him as "dirty, disheveled and a swearing hard drinker." He wound up in a Mob-connected anti-Castro group, which included Jack Ruby. Lee went to Cuba several times, was seen in Havana with Ruby on a couple of occasions, and was interviewed by the FBI three times after coming back from Cuba. They asked him why he went there – he told them it was none of their business. The FBI later denied conducting the interviews.

Lee also was one of two men who wanted to buy ten trucks from a Ford agency in New Orleans on January 20,

1961 for Friends of Democratic Cuba, an organization formed on January 6, 1961, whose Board of Directors included Guy Banister, former head of the Chicago FBI office, former Assistant Superintendent of the New Orleans Police Department and a rabid anti-communist. Also on the Board was Gerard F. Tujague, who had hired Lee as a messenger for his shipping company in 1955, when Lee was sixteen. Lee worked there for a year.

Me and Marina.

As for me, after thirty-three months in Russia, I returned to the U.S. in June of 1962. You're right to wonder why the Russkies let a U.S. defector marry the niece of an MVD colonel and then waltz out of Russia; why the U.S. State Department not only allowed me to come home with no questions asked but even lent me $435 for the trip – in 2016 dollars that's over $3,000; why I was never debriefed, questioned or even met in New York City on my return: not by the State Department, not by the ONI, not by the CIA, not by the FBI – a former U.S. Marine who had 'defected' and had threatened to renounce my citizenship and give secret information to the Soviets about U.S. radar and the U-2 spy plane? No one wanted to talk with me? Doesn't that seen odd?

Actually, I was met by someone – the secretary-general of the American Friends of the Anti-Bolshevik Nations, a private anti-communist operation with extensive U.S. intelligence connections. How did he find me? Why, he was employed by the Traveler's Aid Society of New York City, and some sweet lady in the State Department called and asked him to meet us.

All the same, I couldn't get $200 to fly to Texas with Marina and June – it wouldn't do for a defector to get money from a spy agency, you see. I was pretty steamed about that – finally had to borrow the money from 'brother' Robert.

Doppelgänger: The Legend Of Lee Harvey Oswald

Texas

Marina, June and I flew down to Fort Worth to stay with 'brother' Robert and his wife, but after three weeks he asked us to leave – can't blame him: I wasn't even his brother. Seven days later we moved in with my 'mother,' who had recently come to live in Fort Worth, and after another month we got into our own apartment when I obtained a job, paying $1.25 an hour.

During that time the FBI finally interviewed me. They asked me what I'd done in Russia – I told them not to believe what they read in the papers. They came back in September and asked me to be an informant, which I agreed to. I was given informant number S-172 and paid $200 a month – in cash, of course. But the Agency let me cool my heels, so for a short time I lived an ordinary life. That began to change after George de Mohrenschildt and his wife Jeanne came from Dallas in September to meet us.

George was a White Russian, the son of a Czarist official, and had originally come from Minsk. He traveled around the world as a petroleum engineer, while also doing 'favors' for the CIA, which did him favors in return. The Agency asked George to introduce me and Marina to the White Russian community in Forth Worth and Dallas, through which Marina made some friends. Since George had a Russian background and knew Minsk, the Agency also asked him to finish debriefing me about my stay in Russia.

George later testified that he and I had discussed classical Russian literature – including Tolstoy and Dostoevsky, Jeanne said – *in Russian*, which impressed George. Few people, he noted, could carry on a conversation like that, especially in *fluent, almost accentless Russian*. He later testified that I "had a remarkable fluency in Russian," and that I preferred to read the Russian classics in Russian. He also said I was quite intelligent. Not bad for a tenth-grade dropout from New Orleans.

On October 7, 1962, George came by to urge me to move to Dallas, and the next day I quit my job in Fort Worth, after only two months there. Four days later I had a new job, that George supposedly had arranged for me, paying $1.40 an hour – at Jaggars-Chiles-Stovall, which did sophisticated photographic work, some of it secret work for the government that included putting place names on maps of Cuba used by U-2 pilots. I went to work on October 12, two days before the Cuban missile crisis blew up. A company doing secret government work hires a former Marine who had defected to Russia?

George was my first CIA 'baby-sitter.' A 'baby-sitter' is someone who's assigned to protect and look after an intelligence 'asset.' But George didn't know about the assassination plans – he was just a pawn, like me, in the plotters' deadly game.

I lived in a YMCA, while Marina and June stayed with a friend in Fort Worth. I rented a Dallas P.O. box under my own name (only) at the main Post Office and had my mail forwarded there. On November 4, Marina and June came to live in Dallas, at 604 Elsbeth Street, in the Oak Cliff section, two blocks west of North Beckley Avenue. On November 22 we had the 'family' get-together with Robert, John and their families in Fort Worth. I didn't see my 'brother' Robert – nor my 'mother' – again until the day after JFK's assassination.

In January I finished paying off my State Department loan of $435 – $190 on December 11, $100 on January 9, and $106 on January 29: almost $400 in 1½ months – and I'd also paid off the $200 I'd borrowed from 'brother' Robert. Now, where did I get that money, as I was only paid $1.25 an hour in Fort Worth and $1.40 an hour in Dallas, had worked just six months up to that time?

On February 22, George handed me off to my second 'baby-sitter,' Ruth Paine, at a party he'd arranged so she could meet Marina. Although I didn't know it, Ruth's father had worked for the *Agency for International Development* (AID) – a CIA front company, Ruth herself had gathered intelligence for the CIA in Nicaragua, Ruth's sister Sylvia worked for AID, as did Ruth's brother-in-law.

Ruth was married to Michael Paine, and one of their friends was Fred Osborn, whose father, Fred Sr., was a friend and associate of former CIA Director Allen Dulles. Michael's stepfather, Arthur Young, was the inventor of the Bell Helicopter, and Michael worked at Bell Aerospace Corporation under the war criminal and former Nazi General Walter Dornberger, who was Bell's Director of Research and Development. Ruth and Michael were separated when Marina and I met them.

Of course, I wasn't told about Michael and Ruth's backgrounds. Looking back, it's obvious that Marina and I were moved to Dallas so Ruth could 'baby-sit' us for the Agency.

On March 3, I and Marina and June *supposedly* moved to 214 W. Neely Street. But did we? The Neely Street address was less than a block and a half northwest of our Elsbeth residence. What possible reason would I have for such an odd move, especially since Marina was pregnant and seven weeks later I would go to New Orleans, when Marina and June would go to live with Ruth Paine? I'll discuss this further on.

Later in March I was briefed on creating a chapter of the *Fair Play for Cuba Committee* (FPCC) in New Orleans, as a means of 'sheep-dipping' me – making me appear to be a fervent Castro supporter. So, the 'interest' I'd shown in the Castro revolution while in the Marines came full circle. But, contrary to what the WC tried to maintain later, I didn't order, on January 27 or on March 12 – and didn't receive, at any time – a pistol or a rifle, *supposedly* sent to my P.O. box. More about that later.

At that point the "Oswald Project" merged with the CIA's obsessive efforts to kill Fidel Castro, while also morphing into the conspiracy to terminate JFK, which I wasn't aware of – then. Since the CIA works on a "need to know" basis, I only knew the people I met, the things I did, and what I was told. And, as I found out later, I was quite expendable. I was 'fired' from my job on April 1, my last day of work April 6.

On April 10, someone shot a rifle bullet into the Dallas home of right-wing former General Edwin Walker. Three men and two different cars were seen by two witnesses, before and right after the shooting. The WC later claimed – Marina offering her usual FBI/CIA-concocted lies – that I did it, by myself. But I had no car, no license, didn't drive, wasn't seen, wasn't there. The recovered bullet didn't match 'my' rifle – the one I never bought and never owned. End of story – wasn't me. The tale was meant to show I was a mad killer, capable of assassinating JFK.

I filed for unemployment insurance on April 12 and less than two weeks later left for New Orleans on a bus. It was time to get 'sheep-dipped.' The 'legend' reason for my move was that 'I' was born and grew up in New Orleans and had 'relatives' there. Marina and June stayed in Irving with Ruth, who drove me to the bus depot – what a good 'baby-sitter'! I didn't take with me and didn't later receive 'my' imaginary rifle and pistol.

New Orleans

When I arrived in New Orleans, I called 'Aunt' Lillian and asked if I could stay there for a few days, and she said yes. I went over to their place, and 'Uncle' Dutz drove me to the bus station to pick up my belongings. There was no long package with 'my' imaginary rifle in it among my belongings, though afterward a WC lawyer tried really hard to make Dutz say there was. Later in the day I went out and met David Ferrie, who briefed me and told me my first assignment.

The next morning, as instructed, I followed a young woman named Judyth Vary – a cancer researcher – to the central post office and made sure I got in line behind her at the General Delivery window. She and I would be working with Ferrie and Dr. Mary Sherman on a special project for the next four months. Don't know why they wanted me to meet her like that, but I did. In an odd coincidence, Judyth's grandmother was Hungarian, and Judyth could speak some of the language.

My work then began to move along three parallel paths:

1. Dr. Sherman, Judyth, David and I were tasked with completing the development of a fast-moving cancer, which would be taken to a doctor in Cuba, who would somehow inject Fidel Castro with it. This was one of the far-fetched plots that the CIA dreamed up to kill Castro. Dr. Alton Ochsner, of the Ochsner Clinic in New Orleans, very anti-communist, with close ties to oil man Clint Murchison, was in charge of the project. It was very secret – no paper trail allowed. Dave, Judyth and I worked in Dave's apartment developing cancerous tumors in mice, killed the mice, then handed the tumors over to Dr. Sherman.

2. I needed to publicly represent myself as a strong supporter of Fidel Castro, to give me 'street creds,' so to speak, for any intended trip to Cuba. Keep in mind that Lee Oswald had been to Cuba three or more times in the past, while Castro was coming to power, so the Cubans were aware of Lee, which would be my entrée, since they were meant to think that I was Lee, using a passport photo that was half Lee's face and half mine.

3. I also became involved, too involved for my own good, with the anti-Castro counter-revolutionary plans that were being hatched by Cuban exiles and the Agency. CIA

operative E. Howard Hunt – street name "Eduardo" – had over-all field supervision of this project, but in New Orleans it was controlled by Guy Banister, who'd formerly worked for the ONI, CIA and FBI, and was known to be close to J. Edgar Hoover. Banister had a 'detective agency,' which didn't do much detecting, but he knew about everything covert in New Orleans, including the cancer project. His office – conveniently located near the local ONI, CIA, FBI and Secret Service offices – was also used to store rifles and other military supplies for anti-Castro Cuban exiles.

Meanwhile, I needed to get a regular job to maintain my 'legend.' I was steered to a help-wanted ad of the Reily Coffee Company, which was around the corner from Banister's office and regularly employed CIA assets for short periods of time. William Reily had worked with the CIA for years, and the company's VP was a former FBI agent. Judyth was also sent to Reily's, and we both were hired. One odd thing: Lee's first cousin, William S. Oswald, was a salesman at Reily's.

On May 2, Judyth married Robert Baker, but he worked off-shore most of the time, so little would change in Judyth's life. He left for his job the next day.

On the evening of May 6, Judyth and I were at Dave's apartment when Jack Ruby showed up. A little later Sergio Arcacha-Smith (an anti-Castro leader), William Gaudet (worked with the CIA), and a third man arrived, and we went to a restaurant and had dinner with Carlos Marcello.

Eventually everyone strolled to the home of Clay Shaw, Director of the International Trade Mart in New Orleans and a close friend of Dr. Ochsner. Shaw was a CIA 'asset,' and more. I later learned that, like Banister, he was involved with covert CIA activities in New Orleans. As the others entered Shaw's residence, I and Judyth excused ourselves and went home. Forty-seven years later Judyth wrote a book detailing our relationship in New Orleans and describing this evening.

I started working at Reily's on May 10. A couple of days earlier I'd rented an apartment that a CIA contact had found for me, and on May 11 Ruth drove Marina and June to New Orleans. Everything came together as smooth as silk. Ruth stayed for a few days and then drove back to Irving. Although I was now employed, I continued to collect unemployment insurance from the state of Texas – compliments of the Agency, I assumed.

On June 3, I opened a New Orleans P.O. box, listing a

second name, "A. J. Hidell." A lot of BS has been written about that name, so let me explain. It was a name *given to me after I came to New Orleans*, and it was used not only by me but also by other intelligence operatives. *It was not an alias* – I never used the name as an alternate identity, for anything. *"Hidell" was a project code name* – and it never was on my previous P.O. box application in Dallas because back then I hadn't been given that code name yet. I also used "Alek James Hidell." In Russia people had called me "Alek."

One of those using the code name "Hidell," *and* the variant "Hidel" (along with different first and middle names), was CIA contract agent Richard Case Nagell, who actually had created the "Hidell" name. The different configurations of the name were for different code purposes. More on Nagell later.

I also was still an FBI informant. FBI clerk William Walter, who'd been in the New Orleans FBI office in 1963, told the HSCA that I had "an informant's status with our office." New Orleans bar owner Orestes Pena, an FBI informant himself, said he'd seen "Oswald" on numerous occasions with FBI agent Warren deBrueys. Finally, Adrian Alba, who managed a New Orleans garage next door to Reily's, which housed Secret Service and FBI cars, one day saw me get a white envelope from an FBI car outside, saw me hide it under my shirt, and a few days later saw me once more meet the same car and agent.

In the third week of June, I began my Fair Play for Cuba campaign, writing to the FPCC in New York City to ask for a charter to form a local chapter. I ordered 1,000 handbills locally, which read, "Hands Off Cuba! – Join the Fair Play for Cuba Committee – New Orleans Charter Member Branch – Free Literature, Lectures – Everyone Welcome!" And then I went to the Dumaine Street wharf, where the aircraft carrier U.S.S. Wasp was docked, and handed out handbills to sailors. After a while, harbor police told me to leave.

I continued to juggle my three covert assignments: helping to process tumors from cancerous mice with Judyth in Dave Ferrie's apartment; creating my pro-Castro persona; and getting more and more involved with the anti-Castro operation that was walking in and out of Guy Banister's 'detective agency.' I even had my own 'office' above Banister's and at times also worked near Lake Ponchartrain at a CIA camp that trained Cuban exiles, plus I fell in love with Judyth and began an affair with her.

New Orleans

On June 24, in preparation for a possible trip to Mexico and Cuba, I applied for a new passport – because the old one had too many Russian stamps on it and the picture looked more like Lee than me – and I got it in twenty-four hours! A legitimate one! Made in New Orleans! How's that for service? Of course, I knew the guy who prepared it. There's some perks in working for the Agency.

By the middle of July I'd learned that plans were being made to assassinate JFK, but I couldn't do anything about it. If I talked, I'd be killed, and Marina and Judyth might be too, to teach others a lesson. Over the following years, many men – and women – who knew too much and talked, or planned to talk, *were* murdered to silence them permanently. And having come back from Russia, I was already suspect – I could be a double agent, so the Agency didn't trust me.

Dave Ferrie had been infiltrating the assassination group by loudly and repeatedly saying that Kennedy should be killed. Dave told me and Judyth that Kennedy was doomed if Castro wasn't killed, since the Cuban exiles, the CIA, the Mob, and the military had set their sights on Cuba. If the Cuban revolution could be overthrown by eliminating Fidel Castro with a 'galloping' cancer, JFK might be saved,

Dave said. A slim chance, but better than none.

Dave also believed that what was at stake was not just JFK's life, but the soul of the country. Killing Kennedy would show what happens to anyone who doesn't play ball with the oligarchy, and with Kennedy gone, future governments would exist mostly to create huge profits from extended wars. And one more horror: with JFK eliminated, the likely candidates for the '64 presidential election would be Lyndon Johnson, Barry Goldwater, and George Wallace – and the country could fall into the hands of those who only want more and more money, greater and greater power.

On July 19 I was fired from Reily, since I'd gone missing too many times. Didn't really matter, as I was supposed to leave the next week anyway – easier to just pretend I was looking for work. Soon after I left, four other Reily employees quit and went to work for NASA.

Since my first try to get attention as a Castro supporter by handing out fliers hadn't worked, another plan was hatched. I would again hand out fliers, but this time I'd create some street theatre by staging an altercation and getting arrested, helped by Carlos Bringuier.

Carlos – a Havana-trained lawyer – was a leader in the anti-Castro exile community, the New Orleans delegate of the *Directorio Revolucionario Estudiantil* (DRE), one of the groups most bitter toward JFK. The DRE had been conceived, created and funded by the CIA, and was run by David Atlee Phillips, aka "Maurice Bishop," who earlier had directed raids into Cuba that were designed to force Kennedy into war with Castro. Carlos' job in New Orleans was propaganda and disinformation, at which Phillips was the CIA's top expert. But Phillips was a whole lot more, as I'd soon learn.

So, on August 9, I was again handing out leaflets, this time on Canal Street. There probably were as many intelligence people walking by or watching me as there were regular pedestrians. On cue, Carlos Bringuier rushed up to me with two friends and caused a scene, and we all were taken away by police to be booked. To make sure I'd get an article in the next day's paper, I refused bail and spent the night in jail.

The next morning I asked to see a local FBI agent, and we spoke for an hour and a half – leaving researchers scratching their heads for years afterwards. I was bailed out in the afternoon by a friend of Dutz Murret. Only problem in the whole plan was that I'd stamped on the leaflets the street address of Guy Banister's office as the local FPCC address, and Banister wasn't too happy about that. But no one ever came looking for the FPCC office, no one ever tried to join the FPCC in New Orleans.

On August 16, I handed out leaflets a third time, now in front of the International Trade Mart, with two guys I'd hired for an hour to help me, one an active FBI informant. TV station WDSU, which was friendly with Shaw and Ochsner, was sent to catch my act. We were filmed by a WDSU cameraman who also was an active FBI informant. I stopped handing out leaflets before the cops came, but that night WDSU broadcast a segment about my activities, so now a third of New Orleans knew my name and face – and believed I was a Castro supporter. Fidel's spies were sure to notice.

After my leafleting, a WDSU reporter, Bill Stuckey,

who had a radio show, was told by my handlers to contact me, and the next day I did an interview with him. He broadcast about five minutes of our talk, after which he invited me to participate in a debate four days later with Carlos and three other anti-Communists, plus a second reporter, CIA asset Edward Scannell Butler. I quickly agreed – it was only six against one!

Dr. Ochsner showed up in the studio with us. Now, what was a man like him doing there – a fervent anti-Communist, coming to hear a Marxist like me? Ochsner was friends with several right-wing South American dictators, who also wanted Castro and his Communist crew gone. Ochsner came to make sure I toed the line. I held my ground, though, defending my bogus Marxist views.

All the same, I had no illusions about what was going on. I knew I might be unable to get out of the position I'd been put into, for this group was like the Mob – once you're in, you don't leave it alive. I had to keep playing their game or I'd be dead for sure. Elements of the CIA, the FBI, the Mob, and a lot of 'respectable' people were in bed together – I had nowhere to turn, no one to help me. I was on my own.

Then, much faster than expected, the bioweapon was

ready – a 'galloping' cancer that killed in a short period of time. The cancer had worked not only on mice but on three types of monkeys and now had to be tested on a human. Sort of like the Nazis, but…anything to kill Fidel, thought some in the CIA – Fidel was the 'Red Menace' of the Western Hemisphere, anathema to right-wing dictators, gambling casino operators, the military, and the intelligence community.

A human trial for the cancer was set up for August 29, when a 'volunteer' – a Cuban the same age and build as Castro – from Angola State Penitentiary would be taken to the East Louisiana State Mental Hospital in Jackson and injected with the cancer cells. On that day, Ferrie and I – with the cancer cells in special jars – were driven to Clinton by Clay Shaw in a big black air-conditioned Cadillac owned by the Trade Mart, picking up on the way an orderly who worked at the hospital. We parked by a public phone near the Clinton courthouse, waiting for a call that would tell us when two vehicles transporting the 'volunteer' would be coming by. We would then slip in behind these vehicles and follow them onto the hospital grounds, with the help of the orderly.

There was a delay at Angola, so we had to cool our

heels. I got out of the car and observed a long line of black people waiting to register to vote, which was unexpected. One young woman came out of the registrar's office mad as hell and told me that although she was a college graduate she was refused for 'illiteracy.' I went back to the car and bet Shaw, Ferrie and the orderly that I'd register to vote because I was white, although I didn't live here. They all took the bet, and the orderly got in line with me. We were the only white people.

We waited for about two hours, during which time someone the orderly knew came by and mentioned a job opening at the hospital. When I finally got to the registrar, I "flashed" my ID and signed the roll book, saying I was glad to now be a resident of this parish, which would help with my job application at the hospital. The registrar realized he'd been had, started to erase my name and told me to get out. I went back to the car to collect my bets.

While I was gone, the town marshal walked over to ask Shaw and Ferrie who they were, and Shaw said he was from the Trade Mart and showed the marshal his driver's license. The pay phone finally rang, we drove off to join the convoy, got onto the hospital grounds OK, and the 'volunteer' was given the injection by Ferrie. To create an excuse to return in three days, I filled out an application for the hospital's job opening.

When I got back to New Orleans, I learned that Judyth had made a crucial mistake. Discovering that the 'volunteer' was a completely healthy man, she had written and hand-delivered a note to Ochsner's office, stating that "injecting disease-causing materials" into a healthy man "is unethical." Making a second blunder, she told a secretary the matter was "urgent," and the secretary opened the envelope and conveyed Judyth's comments to Ochsner over the phone when he called in from surgery for messages.

Ochsner was livid, phoning Judyth and screaming that he'd told her there was to be no paper trail, ordering her to never see me again and saying she was finished in medicine, withdrawing his promise to get her into Tulane Medical School in the fall. He then ordered her to Jackson to do tests on the 'volunteer's' blood the next day.

Although Judyth felt crushed, we had already decided to divorce our spouses and get married, meeting in Mexico City after I delivered the cancer cells and then going to South America with a substantial sum from the CIA for all my past work. To help Judyth out now, I gave her $400, the total of my covert pay from the FBI and CIA for the previous month, to tide her over financially.

The next day we went down to Jackson, and Judyth performed the blood tests at the hospital. As we were heading back to New Orleans, Judyth told me she had been given more than one blood sample and she suspected Ferrie had injected more than one man. I agreed he probably had, since three days before he'd asked me to leave the room after the first injection. When we got back, I was told – through Dr. Sherman – that I was not to see Judyth again. Judyth and I both felt a threatening tone to these orders, but we didn't change our plans. We still intended to go to South America.

During the first week of September, I went to Dallas to meet with my CIA handler, along with – supposedly – the Mexico City contact who would see that the cancer cells got into Cuba. When I got to Dallas, "Maurice Bishop" introduced me to another man, whose name I wasn't given, but who was Antonio Veciana. I was told nothing and was immediately sent back to New Orleans, without even lunch, which made me uneasy. Something didn't feel right. Why did "Bishop" want Veciana to see me?

David Atlee Phillips, aka "Maurice Bishop," had been –

and still was in his spare time, although now on an amateur basis – an actor and playwright. From '61 to '63, he had been the CIA's Chief of Covert Action in Mexico City. On September 23, 1963, he was appointed Chief of Cuban Operations. Antonio Veciana had been, at 31, the "boy wonder" of Cuban banking when Castro came to power in '59. He left Cuba and formed Alpha 66, a powerful anti-Castro group (funded by the CIA and supervised by Phillips), which conducted guerrilla attacks and sabotage operations in Cuba in the early 1960s.

Back in New Orleans, a cash account was set up to take care of June and Marina, who was eight months pregnant, and I was told to lay low until the 'volunteer' died, at which time I'd have to be ready to leave at once. On September 17, I picked up a Mexican tourist visa, good until October 2, so that I could go when ordered.

On September 20 CIA contract agent Richard Case Nagell was arrested in El Paso after entering a bank and firing two shots into a wall near the ceiling. He then went outside, sat in his car and waited for the police to arrive. He told an officer that, "I would rather be arrested than commit murder and treason," then added, smiling, "I'm glad you caught me. I really didn't want to be in Dallas."

New Orleans

In the trunk of Nagell's car, among many other items, was a copy of 'Lee Harvey Oswald's' Uniformed Services

Nagell's card didn't have the Defense Department overstamps, another mystery.

ID *with Nagell's picture attached* (above), meaning that Nagell had used, or intended to use, the alias 'Lee Harvey Oswald.' By the way, the picture on *my* card is the right

side of Lee's face and the left side of mine, and the height shown is 5'11", weight 145 lbs. (I was 5'9", 135 lbs., and that's not my chin), meaning that Lee had a copy of the card as well.

Nagell also had a copy of 'Lee Harvey Oswald's' Social Security card and some practice signatures, plus a

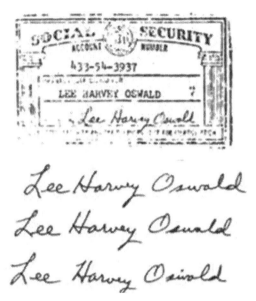

newsletter from the Fair Play for Cuba Committee. If I was "a lone nut," how did Nagell get these? District Attorney Jim Garrison later said, "Richard Nagell is the most important witness there is [to the JFK assassination]."

So, who was this guy? Investigator Dick Russell wrote that Nagell was born in 1930, joined the U.S. Army in 1948, went to Officer Candidate School and became a second lieutenant, was shipped out to the Korean War in 1951, eventually got a battlefield promotion to captain, and wound up with three purple hearts and a Bronze Star. He later was badly hurt in the crash of a B-25, the only survivor. He worked in Army Counter Intelligence, stationed in Japan in the late '50s, and when he finally left that job was an FBI informant, a CIA contract agent, and a Soviet KGB contract agent.

Nagell later said that the KGB assigned him to do surveillance on me in New Orleans, where I met him. Nagell managed to infiltrate the JFK assassination group, reported this to the Soviets, who ordered him to kill me, since the KGB felt that the plotters would try to frame not only me but also the USSR. Nagell decided he wanted out of this bind, so he got himself arrested. Although what Nagell did was a misdemeanor, the government charged him with bank robbery, tried him twice, and kept him locked up for four and a half years before his case was finally thrown out.

A few days before his arrest, Nagell sent J. Edgar Hoover a registered letter, telling him of the coming assassination, my involvement in it, and that he could give the details of the plot, as well as my "real name," to the FBI. Hoover and the FBI denied ever getting such a letter. Nagell was never called to testify by the WC, although he wrote to Senator Richard Russell offering to.

During early September, Marina had been preparing to go with June back to Texas, once more to stay with Ruth Paine in Irving. Ruth arrived on September 20th with her children, and three days later they all left for Texas. While she was in New Orleans, Ruth did not see a rifle or a pistol, nor notice any long package that could have contained a rifle.

Marina later told the FBI she'd never seen me practice with a rifle or any other firearm, that I'd never told her I was going out to practice shooting, either in New Orleans or Dallas, and that she'd never seen boxes of ammunition. That was before she was 'convinced' to say otherwise for the Warren Commission.

'Oswalds' Everywhere

The same day that Ruth and Marina left, September 23, I learned that the 'volunteer' had died and that I should prepare for travel to Mexico City. The following day I met with Clay Shaw and some other men, and was given the bioweapon, along with materials to keep it alive and fresh. Since the bioweapon had to be kept cold, I couldn't travel on hot busses, so I was flown to Mexico on two oil company planes, stopping off along the way in Houston and Dallas, finally landing on a private airstrip in Mexico City two days later.

Now, David Atlee Phillips and his CIA buddies had apparently decided that if two 'Lee Harvey Oswalds' were good, more 'Oswalds' were even better, so – starting in September and right up to November 22 – 'Oswalds' started popping up all over the landscape.

A 'Lee Oswald,' traveling with a man named Hernandez, showed up on Saturday, August 31 in Bacliff, Texas at the door of Robert McKeown – a self-confessed arms dealer who worked in similar circles as Jack Ruby, had supplied arms for Castro's cause, and was a close friend of Castro himself. 'Oswald' said he'd pay $10,000 for four .300 Savage rifles with scopes, rifles which McKeown knew could be bought at Sears and Roebuck for as little as $300 each. McKeown – who'd just come off probation – smelled a rat and turned 'Oswald' away. Could have been Lee.

A man named Perry Russo later told New Orleans District Attorney Jim Garrison that he was at a party, probably on September 15, at which Clay Shaw, David Ferrie, 'Leon Oswald' and some anti-Castro Cubans discussed a plan to kill President Kennedy and blame it on Castro. A few days afterwards, Richard Case Nagell later said, 'Leon' was mistakenly murdered. So, obviously, he wasn't Lee, or me.

On September 25, another 'Lee Harvey Oswald' was at a Selective Service Commission office in Austin, Texas, "attempting to straighten out" his discharge from the Marines, which had been changed from "honorable" to "undesirable" because of his 'defection.' 'Oswald' said he had entered the Marines in Florida and that he lived in Fort Worth. Later that day 'Oswald' was seen in an Austin café.

At 2:35 A.M., September 26 (the same day that I arrived in Mexico City), 'Lee Harvey Oswald' boarded a Continental Trailways bus in Houston, bound for Laredo, Texas. He spoke with other passengers, then took a second bus to Mexico City. On that trip he showed two women his passport, which had Russian stamps on it, i.e., not the new passport I got in June, so that wasn't me either. May have been Lee.

A 'Leon Oswald' showed up on the evening of September 27 at the Dallas apartment of Sylvia Odio, an anti-Castro activist. With him were two Cubans, who introduced themselves as "Angelo" and "Leopoldo." They said they'd just come from New Orleans and were about to go on another trip. They claimed to know Sylvia's father, an anti-Castro activist imprisoned in Cuba, but Sylvia didn't trust them and turned them away.

The next day "Leopoldo" phoned Sylvia and told her that "Leon Oswald" had been in the Marines, was an excellent shot, was "kind of loco," and had said that President Kennedy should have been assassinated for not supporting the Cubans at the Bay of Pigs – that the Cubans should kill him, because he was obstructing freedom for Cuba. A year later the FBI identified "Leon Oswald" as

William Seymour, a member of INTERPEN, who, like Lee Oswald, helped train anti-Castro fighters for the CIA.

Also on September 28, at the Sports Drome Rifle Range in Dallas, Malcolm H. Price, Jr. saw an 'Oswald,' who asked Price to help him adjust the scope on 'Oswald's' rifle – which was a "Mauser-type" with a Japanese scope. 'Oswald' then fired three bullseyes – "a very tight pattern" – into his target. Of course, I was in Mexico City on September 28. Price testified to the WC that he saw 'Oswald' shooting again in mid-October and once more in November, not long before the assassination.

As for me, my contact in Mexico City didn't show. That had never happened to me in all the time I'd worked for the Agency. It was a bad sign – I felt I was being set up for something. What I didn't know then, but know now, is that I *was* being set up, by playwright David Atlee Phillips.

Keep in mind that Phillips was stationed in Mexico City at this time and, being my handler, knew when I was coming there, when I would be absent from New Orleans, so he prepared an elaborate scenario for those days to help frame me. Here's *some* of what happened in Mexico City during that time, *none* of it done by me:

'Oswalds' Everywhere

1. 'Lee Harvey Oswald' went to the Cuban Consulate three times on September 27 and created scenes, demanding a visa to Cuba so he could go to Russia. He was described as five foot six, blond hair, weighing about 125 pounds.

Photo of 'Lee Harvey Oswald' at the Cuban Consulate, provided by the Cuban government.

2. 'Lee Harvey Oswald' *supposedly* made a phone call to the Soviet Embassy in fluent Spanish – I didn't speak Spanish.

3. 'Lee Harvey Oswald' *supposedly* made a phone call to the Soviet Embassy, speaking in broken Russian, "terrible, hardly recognizable Russian" – I spoke fluent Russian.

4. 'Lee Harvey Oswald' twice visited the Soviet Embassy and created scenes there, showing a handgun, demanding a visa to Russia, but never filled out an application. He told them he didn't speak Spanish.

5. 'Lee Harvey Oswald' *supposedly* had a chat at the Soviet Embassy with Valery Kostikov, Russian master assassin.

6. The CIA tapped the phones of the Cuban Consulate and claimed it had tapes of 'Lee Harvey Oswald's' phone calls, then said the tapes had been "routinely recycled." But two FBI agents later listened to copies of the tapes – and reported that the voice on them wasn't mine.

7. The CIA said it had 24/7 automatic photo surveillance of both the Cuban Consulate and the Soviet Embassy, then said the automatic photo equipment hadn't been installed yet when 'Oswald' was there, then said the equipment malfunctioned that weekend, then claimed it didn't do surveillance on weekends, then couldn't produce any pictures of 'Lee Harvey Oswald' but provided the one below to the FBI, showing a white male, 6' tall, athletic

Photo of 'Lee Harvey Oswald,' supposedly taken at the Russian Embassy, provided by the CIA.

build, age about 35, with a receding hairline. Not me.

Had enough of this garbage? There were even wilder claims by the CIA, all of which were proven to be completely false. I had nothing to do with any of it. A 280 page report prepared in 1978 – and classified secret – by the HSCA presented solid CIA evidence that I was impersonated in Mexico City.

Why was it done? To place me in Mexico City, the spy capital of the Western Hemisphere, to show I was connected to Cuba, Castro and the Russians, and that I was sent by Kostikov to kill JFK in Dallas. What I figure is that the original plan was to tie me to the Cubans (my work in New Orleans with the FPCC), but then playwright "Maurice Bishop" overreached himself and added a Russian master assassin to the mix.

The Mexico City charade also was meant to hide the real plot, because when the Washington crowd would later be told that Cuba and the Russians could be involved in JFK's death, they'd stick to the "lone gunman" story come hell or high water, to avert World War III with hydrogen bombs and forty million dead Americans in one hour.

That's why Phillips and his CIA buddies didn't care if

some threads of this fairytale were left dangling – they knew the U.S. government wouldn't risk a legitimate investigation, afraid of what it might uncover. The government wouldn't be able to handle pinning the murder of JFK on Castro, or on Khrushchev, or on the CIA. Brilliant plan, complete with a disinformation booby-trap that no one would dare touch. They even put the FBI in a box, having let the Bureau use me as an informant. If that ever came out, J. Edgar Hoover and all of his lieutenants would be finished, whoever was president.

Bottom line: *everything* reported about me in Mexico City by the CIA was *bogus* – it was *all* part of my 'legend' and designed *to set me up as a patsy* for the murder of JFK! The Mexico City masquerade was a second-rate Hollywood story so bad that no one but the CIA would have produced it. If all this hadn't been so deadly serious – tragic – it would've been hilarious: Buster Keaton in Mexico City. Yet it served its purpose for the plotters.

I didn't know about any of that, but I did know that my Mexico City trip was a disaster:

1. my contact failed to show up,

2. my role in the bioweapon plot was finished,

3. when I tried reaching Phillips in Mexico City, I learned he'd flown to Washington D.C. two days earlier,

4. the pilot who'd agreed to fly Judyth to Mexico City, Alex Rorke, a good friend, was reported missing on a flight,

5. there now was no way to get my CIA back pay to go to South America with Judyth,

6. and I was ordered to return, to Dallas – I didn't know for what.

Doppelgänger: The Legend Of Lee Harvey Oswald

Back To Dallas

Meanwhile, Lee Oswald had been working for the CIA in Florida on anti-Castro projects, which included training fighters in the Everglades, and he also became part of Operation 40, a top secret CIA project for selected Cuban exiles to learn guerrilla warfare aimed at the Castro regime. Some of the recruits were specially instructed to do assassinations. One of these, a woman named Marita Lorenz, said she trained with Lee Oswald and knew him as "Ozzie." She didn't like him, thought he was "a creep."

In the summer of '63, while I was living in New Orleans, Lee was in Dallas. Jack Ruby's girlfriend, Dorothy Marcum, remembered that Lee worked for Ruby for a couple of months then. Mechanic Robert Roy said Lee often drove Ruby's car back and forth from his garage. Lee had a conversation with Frances Hise in Ruby's Carousel Club – a strip joint – and offered to buy her a drink. On another occasion Hise noticed Lee come in the back door of the club and heard Ruby say, "Hi, Ozzie" – Ruby later joined "Ozzie" in a back room. Ruby employees William Crowe, Wally Weston, Dixie Lynn, Kathy Kay and others said they saw Lee in Ruby's club. Bill DeMar told FBI agents that he saw "Oswald" in the Carousel eight or ten days before the assassination.

Beverly Oliver, a singer at the nearby Colony Club, became friends with Carousel dancer "Jada." One evening in early November Beverly went into the Carousel and saw Jada and Jack Ruby sitting at a table with a young man. When she walked over to them, Jack rose and said, "Beverly, this is my friend Lee Oswald. He's with the CIA." Beverly later said she found the man disturbing. Soon after the assassination, Jada, speaking to reporters, also told about meeting "Oswald."

Jack Hammond, manager of the Delux Diner #1, 315 S. Ervay Street (6 blocks southeast of the Carousel Club, 14 from where I would work) later told the FBI that in October and November "Lee Harvey Oswald" would come into the diner and order french fries. That was Lee, of course.

On October 3, I was back in Dallas, 'looking for work,' and took a room at a YMCA. On October 4, I hitchhiked out to Irving to see Marina and June, stayed the weekend, and then caught a bus back to Dallas. I rented a room for $7 a week at 621 North Marsalis Avenue, in the Oak Cliff section (nine blocks north of Jack Ruby's apartment) from Mrs. Mary Bledsoe. Much later it was learned that Mrs. Bledsoe's son knew David Ferrie, having been trained in the Civil Air Patrol by Ferrie. Saturday morning, October 12, Mrs. Bledsoe told me to leave – she'd taken a dislike to me, she told the WC.

I went out to Irving again and was driven back to Dallas by Ruth Paine on Monday *morning, October 14*, when I rented a room at 1026 North Beckley Avenue, seven blocks northwest of Marsalis Avenue, seven blocks northeast from Elsbeth Street. The housekeeper at 1026 was Mrs. Earlene Roberts, whose sister, Bertha Cheek, not only knew Jack Ruby but at one time had looked into investing in Ruby's Carousel Club. A former boarder of Ms. Cheek was police officer Harry N. Olsen, who later married a Carousel Club stripper. Another tenant in 1026, John Carter, was friends with longtime friend and ex-employee of Ruby, Wanda Killam.

In the evening I supposedly was told about a possible job. The cover story for this was that on the *afternoon* of October 14, Mrs. Lynn Randle, a neighbor who lived down the block (Ruth lived at 2515 West Fifth Street), told Ruth

Paine about the *Texas School Book Depository* (TSBD), where Mrs. Randle's brother Buell Wesley Frazier worked, and Ruth *supposedly* relayed this info to me by phone that evening. I applied for a job *the next day*, and TSBD superintendent Roy S. Truly said they could use me "for a brief time" and hired me. Curiously, he had laid off eight workers the day before I was hired.

The real story about my hire is that this was another CIA-arranged temporary job, like Jaggars-Chiles-Stovall in Dallas and Reily's in New Orleans. TSBD superintendent Truly (who also was a member of the TSBD board of directors), was told I was working undercover for the FBI, which I was and which he never disclosed. This throws a whole new light on Truly and the TSBD, as events unfolded.

The TSBD company only procured its seven-story building at 411 Elm Street a year before the assassination, substantially renovated it, and *moved in sometime during the summer of 1963*. That adds another layer of strangeness to the TSBD.

In November, 1963, the building had three elevators. There was a passenger elevator near the southeast corner, which for some reason only went up to the fourth floor. In the northwest corner were a flight of steps going to the seventh floor, which employees were told not to use, as the steps supposedly needed repair. (Why weren't they fixed when the building was renovated?) East of the staircase, against the north wall, were two freight elevators. One of these, the west elevator, had a gate that had to be lowered for the elevator to function. When the gate was down, this elevator could be summoned from another floor. The east elevator did not have a gate and could not be summoned.

The building, at the corner of Houston Street, was owned by Dallas oilman David Harold Byrd, cousin of conservative U.S. Senator Harry F. Byrd. D. H. Byrd had a close relationship with both Lyndon Johnson and Texas Governor John Connally, was an oil associate of Sid Richardson and Clint Murchison, knew George de Mohrenschildt and may have known David Atlee Phillips through the Dallas Petroleum Club, of which George H. W. Bush also was a member.

After Johnson became president, Byrd's aircraft company, LTV, received a large defense contract – in January, 1964 – to build fighter planes for Vietnam. The previous November, Byrd had teamed up with his LTV partner James Ling to buy 132,000 shares of LTV stock. Although required by SEC rules to report this insider purchase, they delayed doing so until well after JFK's death.

I started my job at the TSBD on Wednesday, October 16. I was trained to fill the orders of publishing company Scot, Foresman and Co., whose books were on the first and sixth floors, so I spent a lot of time working on the sixth floor. No time cards were used for the warehouse workers, and they were paid in cash.

After work on Friday, Wesley Frazier gave me a ride out to Irving, so I could again see June and Marina, who was almost ready to give birth to our second child. On Sunday, October 20, Audrey Rachel Oswald was born. I didn't expect to see her grow up – it was looking more and more like I'd be done away with. I'd learned that Alex Rorke – a former Jesuit priest – was dead, shot down over Cuba by the CIA because he wouldn't go along with the assassination.

By now I'd been pulled into the actual assassination planning. I discovered that there were four alternate assassination sites: Chicago, Miami, Dallas, and Los Angeles. Each site would have a patsy, a feature invented by the Sicilian Mafia centuries ago.

Chicago actually became operational. On Wednesday, October 30, at 9:00 A.M., the Chicago Secret Service office was notified by the FBI of a plot to assassinate JFK on November 2 along the route of a Chicago presidential motorcade. Four snipers planned to shoot JFK in an ambush with high-powered rifles. The Agent in Charge told his men that the intelligence had come from an FBI informant named "Lee."

The next day the landlady of a North Side boardinghouse called the FBI to report that four men had rented rooms from her, in which she'd seen four rifles with telescopic sights, as well as a newspaper sketch of the president's route. The FBI refused to get involved, told the Secret Service this was their jurisdiction.

The four men were put under surveillance, and two were soon taken into custody. They wouldn't answer questions, were released after November 2, and have remained anonymous; the other two suspects were never found. JFK's parade was cancelled at the last moment, and he did not come to Chicago.

However, a patsy was apprehended: an ex-Marine named Thomas Arthur Vallee, who was found to have two rifles and twenty-five hundred rounds of ammunition in his rented room. Vallee, who signed up with the Marines at age fifteen in 1948 and was badly wounded in Korea, had a metal plate in his head, was a loner, a paranoid schizophrenic, and on complete disability from the VA. His sister said he'd been "set up." It later was learned that Vallee had helped the CIA, at a camp near Levittown, Long Island, to train Cuban exiles to assassinate Fidel Castro, just like Lee Oswald was doing in Florida. At the time of Vallee's arrest, the license plate number of his car was classified – restricted to U.S. intelligence. Another "lone nut" CIA operative.

Meanwhile, David Atlee Phillips and his boys were again busy providing bogus 'Lee Harvey Oswalds' all over the Dallas area:

1. On November 1, an 'Oswald' bought ammunition for a rifle (not a Carcano) at Morgan's Gun Shop in Fort Worth. A witness told the FBI that 'Oswald' was rude and impertinent, made a point of saying he'd been in the Marine Corps. When the witnesses later saw the man's picture in *Life*, they agreed that he was "Lee Harvey Oswald." Except he wasn't me.

2. The next day, November 2, 'Lee Oswald' came into a Lincoln Mercury dealership near Dealey Plaza, wanting

to buy a red Mercury, said he'd get the car for all cash in two or three weeks. He then went on a wild test drive, speeding at up to 75-85 mph. When told he needed a credit rating to buy the vehicle, 'Oswald' replied, "Maybe I'm going to have to go back to Russia to buy a car." Only problem: I didn't drive, had no driver's license and was somewhere else that afternoon.

3. On November 10th and 17th, Garland G. Slack saw an 'Oswald' at the Dallas Sports Dome, a rifle range. On the 17th, 'Oswald' deliberately provoked Slack by repeatedly and rapidly firing at Slack's target, even though Slack objected strenuously. However, on November 10 I was at Ruth Paine's place, so it wasn't me either.

Notice that all of these 'Oswalds' acted in obnoxious ways, which was meant to draw attention to them and also feed into the part of my 'legend' that I was an angry and disturbed person. And how did I get to all these places, if I had no car and didn't drive?

On the evening of November 14, a witness later reported, he saw Jack Ruby with Dallas Police Officer J. D. Tippit in Ruby's Carousel Club (1312½ Commerce Street, eight blocks southeast of the TSBD), along with a third man named Bernard Weissman, and that the three were talking together for more than two hours. Jack's sister, Eva Grant, told the *New York Herald Tribune* that both she and Jack knew Tippit, that "Tippit used to come into the Vegas Club and Carousel Club," and that Jack "called him buddy." At least six witnesses, including Dallas Police Lieutenant George C. Arnett, confirmed that Jack Ruby knew Tippit.

Robert "Tosh" Plumlee, then a CIA contract pilot, has written that J. D. Tippit – and Roscoe White, another employee of the Dallas Police Department – were members of a special DPD tactical team that would operate in support of U.S. intelligence operations, esp. the 112th Military Intelligence Group, which worked with the ONI.

White, who was hired by the DPD only on October 7, 1963 as a clerk-photographer, had been a Marine and was on the U.S.S. Bexar at the same time as Lee Oswald when both shipped out. White may have been an intelligence operative, black ops, reaching back to his Marine days. His wife, Geneva, was a dancer at the Carousel Club, and White was said to know Jack Ruby well.

At 1:45 A.M. on November 17, a telegram was received by the New Orleans FBI office from J. Edgar Hoover, stating that the "Bureau has determined that a military revolutionary group may attempt to assassinate President Kennedy on his…trip to Dallas…November 22-23….Other offices have been advised….." Isn't that interesting? "A military revolutionary group." So, were the White House and Secret Service also "advised"? Was the Dallas FBI office? Do you wonder who gave this warning to J. Edgar?

On Wednesday, November 20, Officer J. D. Tippit was having coffee at the Dobbs House Restaurant, 1221 N. Beckley (southwest corner of Beckley and Colorado), in Oak Cliff, two blocks north of my rooming house, *as was his habit about that time most mornings*, a waitress said, when another man, also a regular customer, started complaining loudly about his order of eggs. Tippit glanced twice at the man but said nothing. Lee gave this performance so Tippit would recognize me later on.

The waitress' statement that Tippit was in the restaurant, "as was his habit about the same time most mornings," is very curious. Dobbs House was *just over six miles* northwest from *the closest point* of Tippit's assigned patrol district, #78. Under normal driving conditions, it would have taken Tippit about *forty-five minutes* round trip from his assigned district to Dobbs House. Why would he come there for a coffee break *"most mornings"*?

The noisy customer was later identified by the owner and employees as "Lee Harvey Oswald." Waitress Mary Dowling reported that "Oswald" had *usually eaten breakfast* at the restaurant between 7:00 and 7:30 A.M. *(But Marina testified that I <u>never</u> had breakfast – I didn't like to eat in the morning!)* Lee apparently lived just a few blocks from my rooming house, in order to confuse the record even more.

Waitress Dowling recalled that "Oswald" was last seen by her in the restaurant that morning at about 10:00 A.M., at which time he was "nasty" and used curse words. Notice that, like in earlier events, "Oswald" was obnoxious. I was at work at 8:00 A.M. that morning, so that wasn't me.

"Tosh" Plumlee later wrote that there was "an Oak Cliff safe house on North Beckley Street run by Alpha 66's Hernandez group, which had worked out of Miami prior to the assassination." So then all the "Oswald" sightings in Oak Cliff would indicate that Lee Oswald had lived at that "safe house" for a while before the assassination.

Plumlee also wrote that he had met Lee Harvey Oswald on a number of occasions connected with intelligence training in the past, including at Illusionary Warfare Training in Nagshead, North Carolina, in Honolulu at a radar installation, and in Dallas at the Oak Cliff safe house. That was Lee he met, of course.

Shortly after the Dobbs House incident, at 10:30 A.M., Ralph Leon Yates, a refrigeration mechanic, was driving his pickup truck on the Thornton Expressway when he noticed a man hitchhiking in Oak Cliff near the Beckley Avenue onramp. Yates decided to pick him up.

When the hitchhiker got into the truck, he was carrying "a package about 4 feet to 4 1/2 feet long," covered with brown wrapping paper. Yates told him he could put the package in the back of the pickup, but the man replied that the package contained curtain rods and he'd rather keep it in the cab. The hitchhiker, Yates later said, looked so much like Lee Harvey Oswald that he seemed to be Oswald's double.

Yates mentioned to 'Oswald' that people were getting excited about the president's upcoming visit, and 'Oswald' then asked Yates "if he thought a person could assassinate the President" with a rifle from the top of a building or out of a window, high up. He showed Yates a photo of a man holding a rifle. 'Oswald' also asked if Yates thought the President might change his parade route (the parade route was changed at the last minute to go past the TSBD). Yates dropped 'Oswald' off at the stoplight by Elm and Houston and last saw 'Oswald' carrying his package of "curtain rods" over to the TSBD side of Elm Street.

After Yates saw pictures of me in the media, he said the man he gave the ride to was "identical with Oswald." That 'Oswald's' comments were – like the behavior of other 'Oswalds' in the self-incriminating incidents already seen – a blatant attempt to draw attention to 'Lee Harvey Oswald' as a potential presidential assassin. This obviously was the same 'Oswald' who was in the Dobbs House Restaurant – someone must have picked him up in a car after his explosive display, driven him to the freeway and handed him the "curtain rods" package. I was at work then.

I'd kept in touch with Judyth by phone, and that evening I called and told her the JFK ambush would go down on Friday afternoon, but I didn't give her any details, since that would have put her life in danger. I did say I expected to be killed by the plotters, and that I was convinced my CIA handler's real name was David Atlee Phillips. I told Judyth to remember that name – he was the traitor running the operation. I never spoke with her again.

The next afternoon, Thursday, November 21, I broke my weekly routine and asked Wesley for a ride out to

Irving after work. I wanted to be with my two little girls one more time – I had a feeling I'd never see them again after Friday. I played with them that evening and afterwards put $170 in a dresser drawer for Marina, what was left of my FBI pay from the previous month. I'd been paid only $208.82 by the TSBD over the five weeks I'd worked there – I couldn't have saved $170. I also put my gold wedding ring in a ceramic cup on the dresser. I didn't expect to be coming back.

Where was Lee Oswald? Around 2:15 A.M., November 22, head waitress Mary Lawrence, who had known Jack Ruby for the past eight years, was working at the Lucas B & B Restaurant, two doors down from Jack Ruby's Vegas Club. Lawrence said "Lee Harvey Oswald" entered the restaurant and told her and the night cashier that he was waiting for Jack Ruby. When Ruby came in, the two men sat together, talked for over half an hour and then left.

She reported this to the Dallas police and ten days later received an anonymous phone call from a man who told her, "If you don't want to die, you better get out of town." Questioned by police, Lawrence stuck to her story, stating that the man with Ruby was "positively Lee Harvey Oswald." And it was! The real one!

Doppelgänger: The Legend Of Lee Harvey Oswald

Friday, November 22, 1963

We now come to assassination day. Before I continue, I want you to *remember from now on that on this day I was wearing a <u>rust-brown</u> tweed shirt with a pattern, all of its top buttons ripped off (<u>before</u> I was arrested), right elbow ripped out*, and a T-shirt pulled into a V-neck. Below are pictures of the shirts:

Warren Commission Exhibit 150.

Co-worker Charles Douglas Givens remembered that I wore a brown, long sleeved shirt that day, so did Mary Bledsoe when I got on the Marsalis bus, so did cab driver William Whaley when he drove me to Oak Cliff.

My day began with Buell Wesley Frazier, so let's take a closer look at him. Wesley, 19, came to Irving from Huntsville, Texas during the early part of September, 1963 and moved in with his sister, Lynn Randle, her husband, and her three children, at 2439 W. 5th Street. Wesley said he got his job with the TSBD on September 13, 1963 through an Irving employment agency, a statement never checked by the WC. The TSBD was about fifteen miles from the Randle house.

Friday, November 22, 1963

Asked by the WC when he "first heard" I'd been hired by the TSBD, Wesley replied, "Talking back and forth with the bossman all the time and from being around and getting along real fine – and so he told me." Why would fifty-six-year-old superintendent Roy Truly tell a nineteen-year-old $1.25 an hour order filler who'd worked there only two months about a new temporary worker Truly had hired just that day? Truly didn't work on the floor but in his private office. All the same, testified Wesley, "I knew, you know, that [Lee] was going to be coming to work." I was hired on October 15th and went to work the next morning, so how and when did Wesley learn I'd been hired?

Wesley testified he'd also learned about my hire from his sister "Linnie Mae," who "found out from one of the neighbors." What neighbor? Linnie Mae testified she'd only ever met Ruth Paine twice, once a year earlier and then *supposedly* on October 14, when she *supposedly* mentioned the TSBD and her brother to Ruth, and I was hired the following day.

Linnie Mae, questioned by the WC if Ruth Paine had told her that Lee didn't have a job, replied, "Well, I suppose," then added, "It was just general knowledge in the neighborhood that he didn't have a job." General knowledge? When I didn't live there and had only made two recent weekend visits to Irving, after being in New Orleans for the past five months? Why would Ruth Paine blab all over the neighborhood that I was out of work, as soon as I got to Dallas?

Did Linnie Mae know Lee had been hired by the TSBD? "I didn't even know that he had even tried any place." Did she later learn that Lee had applied for a job? "Mrs. Paine told me, *later*, that he had applied for the job and had gotten the job." (Wait a minute, didn't Linnie Mae testify that the only time she'd met Ruth in 1963 was on October 14?) And then did she tell Wesley that "a fellow named Lee Oswald" was going to work for the TSBD? "No, sir, I didn't even know his name." But had she told Wesley about Lee getting the job? "Sir, I don't remember if I mentioned it to him or not.... I might have had. But I can't say for sure I did, because at the time it was unimportant to me." Does this sound like someone who's telling the truth or recalling *anything*? Or does it sound like she hadn't been prepped on this topic by the FBI and WC?

Wesley testified that when I came to work at the TSBD on the 16th, "Talking back and forth [with Lee], he come to find out I knew his wife was staying there at the time with

Friday, November 22, 1963

this other woman." What a coincidence! But how did Wesley find that out? He said he didn't know Ruth Paine, and his sister had only met Ruth one time that year, two days earlier.

And when the WC asked Truly if I had struck up any friendships or acquaintanceships with other employees, Truly replied, "I never saw [Lee] with anyone else, except…maybe asking where books were…. But very little conversation he had with anyone. And he worked by himself…. Consequently, he didn't have much occasion to talk with the other boys." Everyone said I was quiet and didn't talk much.

And Wesley also testified that I spoke very little during the times he drove with me to Irving and back. And other TSBD employees testified that I always ate lunch alone, usually reading. So, how did Wesley "talk back and forth" with me during my first two days at the TSBD? Fact is, though, Wesley gave me a ride to Irving that Friday afternoon, October 18. Wasn't it convenient that Wesley lived only half a block from Ruth – what are the odds on that?

Then, Wesley claimed I drove with him to Irving Thursday night, November 21, to get some curtain rods for

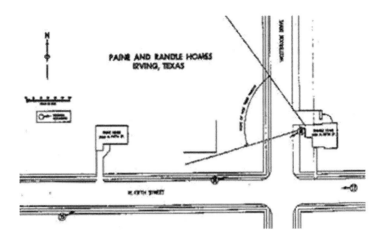

Warren Commission Exhibit 440 – Paine home left, Randle home right.

my Dallas "apartment," and that when I came for my ride Friday morning I placed a package, which I told him were "curtain rods," on the back seat of his car. He said the package was about 27" long – or 11" shorter than the paper bag the WC later claimed 'my' disassembled rifle had been wrapped in.

Linnie Mae also said she saw me place a 27" package on the back seat of Wesley's car, "He opened *the right back door*, and I just saw that he was laying the package down." Only problem with that observation is that it wasn't possible to see what she described from her kitchen door, where she claimed she was standing, because a partition of the carport hid Wesley's car from the house, plus it was a cloudy day, right after dawn. And just why did she even

Friday, November 22, 1963

look out the door? Wesley had told her who I was when she saw me through her kitchen window. Not only that, but Essie Mae Williams, Linnie Mae's mother, told the FBI that she saw me coming, through the kitchen window, and that I had nothing in either of my hands. She wasn't called to testify.

West side of Randle house, showing the carport and location of Wesley's car as it was on the morning of November 22.

Wesley's car from the right side.

In any case, the WC couldn't make those stories work, especially the 27" length of my imaginary package, containing an imaginary rifle, since Wesley testified I had one end of the package cupped in my right hand and the other end in my armpit – a length of about 21" – as I *supposedly* carried it into the TSBD. However, TSBD employee Jack Dougherty, who was sitting on the wrapping table near the back door, where I came in, insisted he didn't see me carry *anything* into the building that morning, nor did anyone else, at any time that day.

There was no such package, I never told Wesley that I was getting or bringing curtain rods to the TSBD, and I told the police that when I was arrested. Of course, I was killed on November 24, so Wesley could say whatever the FBI wanted him to. So could Linnie Mae.

Anyway, nothing significant happened with me before noon that day. After Dougherty saw me come in at 8:00, he and two or three people saw me filling orders that morning. Shortly before 11:50, Bill Shelley, manager of the Miscellaneous Department, and his crew laying plywood flooring on the sixth floor quit for lunch and went down in the two freight elevators. I was on the fifth floor and yelled at them to lower the gates on the west elevator when they

Friday, November 22, 1963

got to the bottom so I could call that elevator back up. Several of the men on the elevator heard me.

Bill Shelley testified he saw me at 11:50 near a phone on the first floor, which means he and his crew stopped working around 11:45. Packer Eddie Piper told the Sheriff's department that I was on the first floor at 12:00 and said to him, "I'm *going up* to eat." That was to the second floor lunchroom, which had vending machines. Another place warehouse workers ate was the domino room on the first floor, at the northeast corner overlooking the loading dock, but that room had no vending machines.

Shortly before, probably between 11:00 and 11:30, two teams of shooters probably climbed the fire escape – on the east wall of the TSBD – to the roof. Three of the men wore suits or sport coats and likely had fake Secret Service credentials in case they were challenged. They might even have taken their rifles up with them, since other men had been seen carrying rifle cases in Dealey Plaza without alarm, as people thought they were Secret Service. A 'policeman' might have been on the sidewalk below, should anyone question who they were.

Knowing that the TSBD workers would have left the sixth floor for lunch, the assassins went down the stairs

Firing positions at far southwest and southeast windows. Outside dimensions of the TSBD are 100' X 110'.

from the roof to their firing positions on the sixth floor after 11:50, but how could they be sure no one was now there? Bill Shelley made sure.

Carolyn Arnold, secretary of TSBD Vice President O. V. Campbell, went into the second floor lunchroom "...about 12:15, *it may have been later....* Oswald was sitting in one of the booth seats on the right-hand side of

Friday, November 22, 1963

the room as you go in. He was alone as usual and appeared to be having lunch. I did not speak to him but I recognized him clearly." She knew me because in the past I'd come to her desk on the second floor looking for change. She and friend Virgie Rackley went down "about 12:15," Virgie said.

Truly and Campbell left the building around 12:15 to see JFK, stood about 20 feet in front of the TSBD. Mrs. Robert A. Reid, a clerical supervisor who worked in the second floor offices went to stand near Truly. Bill Shelley, Billy Lovelady and Wesley Frazier drifted out.

The Texas School Book Depository, seen from Houston Street, Dealey Plaza to the left.

Vickie Adams, Sandra Styles and two other women walked to the third set of windows west of Houston on the fourth floor to watch the motorcade. Having finished eating, I walked downstairs and went outside a couple of minutes after 12:20, standing on the third step from the bottom of the entryway, leaning against the column on my right.

TEXAS SCHOOL BOOK DEPOSITORY
DIAGRAM OF FOURTH FLOOR

Back stairs
West and east elevators
HOUSTON STREET
Passenger elevator
Where Vickie Adams stood
ELM STREET

Vickie Adams' position.

Some spectators south of Elm Street saw two men in

Friday, November 22, 1963

the sixth floor far southwest windows of the TSBD, one similar in appearance to "Lee Harvey Oswald" (one witness saw them at 12:15, when I was eating), a couple of witnesses saw a man in the sixth floor far southeast windows. Up to twenty inmates at the county jail on Houston Street saw two men for several minutes in the sixth floor far southwest windows with a rifle that had a scope. All witnesses reported that the younger man, about 25, in the southwest windows was wearing a light-colored shirt. There were *no* reports of a man wearing a rust-brown long-sleeved tweed shirt in any of the windows.

Dallas County Sheriff Bill Decker ordered his men *not* to provide *any* security for the motorcade. Abandoning standard procedure, windows on buildings around the plaza were *not* sealed by the Secret Service. The 112th Army Intelligence Unit, based at Fort Sam Houston, Texas and highly trained for presidential protection, was emphatically ordered by superiors in the Pentagon to *stay away* – despite bitter protests from its commander. So, there were *no* sharpshooters on the surrounding rooftops, *no* soldiers doing crowd control in Dealey Plaza.

Two motorcycle policemen on both sides of JFK's limousine, standard in all presidential motorcades, *were missing*. The Secret Service agents normally assigned to stand on footholds at the rear fenders of the presidential limousine were ordered off their special stands just as the motorcade began – they might have been able to save the president's life.

The original route of the motorcade had been straight down Main Street, which was parallel to Elm, then under the triple underpass and onto a freeway, moving at a rate of 44 miles per hour as dictated by Secret Service regulations. Instead, in the previous two days the route was changed, now turning right on Houston Street and left on Elm, a 120 degree turn, driving at under 11 miles an hour into a perfect ambush site.

Ambush

At 12:30:47 P.M., Central Time, John Fitzgerald Kennedy, 35th President of the United States, driving west on Elm Street in Dallas, Texas, came under fire from several directions and was shot to death in a military-style ambush that was conceived by a cabal and was overseen by CIA renegades.

This photo, Altgens6, by James Altgens, taken just as the first shot was fired, shows how close the Secret Service agents were to JFK and how they did not move, while Johnson's agents were already opening the door of their car.

When the shooting began, Secret Service agents were

ordered by the agent in charge to stay in their car, which was only a few feet behind the presidential limousine, so President Kennedy received *no protection whatever from the Secret Service*. Only Clint Hill, Jacqueline Kennedy's personal agent, ignored that order and sprinted from the Secret Service car to protect the First Lady. The president's car was moving less than ten miles an hour, at the first shot slowed to a crawl and finally came to a momentary *stop*, allowing the assassins to inflict the fatal head shots. In short, there were a lot of traitors in Dallas and in Washington D.C. on November 22. I wasn't one of them.

Two teams of shooters/spotters were on top of the "grassy knoll," behind a stockade fence. A witness said he saw a man who was middle aged or older, fairly heavy set, in a white shirt and dark trousers, not far from a second man, younger, about mid-twenties, in either a plaid shirt or plaid coat or jacket.

The young man may have been James Files, who years later said he had fired the last, fatal, shot and had worn a plaid poplin jacket. Files claimed that while in the Army as a young man he had been recruited into CIA operations by David Atlee Phillips, that Phillips was his control and had given him the weapon he used to shoot JFK – the

Remington Fireball XP-100 – and that Files used a mercury-filled bullet, which exploded JFK's head.

Files said he had driven to Texas a week before the assassination and had stayed at a motel in Mesquite [14 miles from Dallas]. Files: "The following day, Lee Harvey Oswald came by...and he took me out to...somewhere southeast of Mesquite where I test fired the weapons and calibrated the scopes.... Then he was with me for a few days in town there [Dallas]....We drove around...so I would know all the streets." That was Lee, of course – I couldn't have been with Files. Earline Roberts testified I was in my room all that weekend, and I was at work every day the next week.

The second shooting team on the "grassy knoll" was dressed as Dallas policemen, one of whom might have been 32-year-old Corsican assassin Lucien Sarti, known to wear disguises like police uniforms. A third man – dressed like a rail worker – broke apart and took away his team's rifle in a satchel.

There were two men dressed in suits, who carried forged Secret Service credentials. When people ran up to where these men were after the shots, the 'Secret Service men' and the 'Dallas policemen' controlled the scene. Later, the Secret Service and the Dallas police both denied having any men on the "grassy knoll," either before or immediately after the shooting.

Standing on the steps of the "grassy knoll's" pergola moments after the shots, Beverly Oliver – in Dealey Plaza to take motion pictures of JFK – saw Roscoe White hurriedly cross in front of her, dressed in his police uniform but without his police hat or pistol. Some people believe White was one of the "grassy knoll" shooters.

At the TSBD sixth floor far southwest windows were Lee Oswald and his spotter, at the southeast TSBD windows was another shooter/spotter team. There was a team inside the Dal-Tex Building on the southwest end of its second floor. There was a shooter on top of the Records Building (southeast corner of Elm and Houston), possibly a shooter in a storm sewer drain at the base of the steps on the north side of Elm Street, and a shooter on the South

Knoll, at the far right.

"Tosh" Plumlee has written he was part of an "abort" team sent to Dallas to prevent a squad of *at least twenty people* from assassinating JFK in Dealey Plaza. Plumlee wrote that his team was attached to a military intelligence unit and supported by the CIA – that its information had come from sources in Texas and the CIA. When the shooting began, Plumlee was on the South Knoll. He heard four or five shots, one fired from behind and to his left on the South Knoll, near the underpass and south parking lot.

In addition to the shooters and spotters, there was "the umbrella man," who triggered the shots, a radio man communicating with a command post somewhere not far off, and a photographer to take "trophy" photographs. Others, who knew what was coming, such as Jack Ruby, were in Dealey Plaza to watch. There could have been as many as 30-35 people connected with the plot in and around the plaza, including getaway vehicles with drivers.

There were 10-12 shots, at least 4 striking JFK (the last two were almost simultaneous shots to the rear and front of his head), 2 shots hitting Texas Governor John Connally, who was sitting in front of JFK. Three shots – probably the first, second and fourth – came from the TSBD. The rear head shot likely came from the Dal-Tex Building. The fourth Kennedy shot – the frontal head shot – came from the "grassy knoll." Up to fifty-one witnesses – including policemen, Secret Service agents, sheriff's deputies, reporters and two JFK aides – reported they heard one or two shots from the front. Some witnesses also smelled gunpowder in the street. The lines in the photograph below show some of the likely trajectories.

To disguise how many shooters there were, as many as four rifles may have had silencers attached to them, so the *explosions* of shots from those weapons were not *heard* – although where some struck the ground could later be *seen*. The *explosions* of the shots *heard* from the TSBD were to frame "the lone nut" shooter and to make people look toward the TSBD, helping to disguise the subsequent shots.

The kill shot from the "grassy knoll," from the Fireball, which had no silencer, was to be fired *only* if JFK were not already dead, which is why *that* shot was heard by many. Other bullets were heard only as they broke the sound barrier. One man on the "grassy knoll" *felt* the shock wave of a bullet as it passed near his left shoulder from the rear.

In order to tie the 'three shots' fired at JFK to 'my' Italian 6.5mm Carcano rifle, some of the bullets had previously been fired into water from 'my' Carcano, retrieved, put into sabots, then fired at JFK – to frame me.

A bullet with a plastic sabot around it, in its casing.

A sabot is a plastic jacket which is placed around a bullet that's smaller than its casing. The sabot protects the bullet's original rifling marks, so that investigators recovering the bullet will think it came from the original weapon, complete with the original rifling marks – in this case, from 'my' Carcano. A sabot reportedly was found on the ground in Dealey Plaza on the afternoon of November 22 by a civilian, and in 1975 a casing with a crimp around its edge, indicating that a sabot had been used, was found on the roof of the Records Building.

Lee Oswald fired one or two shots, immediately handed his 7.65 Mauser to his spotter, quickly walked to the rear stairs and started down, as his spotter hid the rifle between some boxes. Since I worked on the sixth floor, anyone noticing Lee come down the stairs – wearing a T-shirt – would think it was me. The shooter in a southeast window also fired one or two rounds, took his rifle with him, then he and his spotter followed Lee's spotter and hid their rifle. There were people downstairs on the fourth and fifth floors, which made it too risky for three strange men to go down the stairs after Lee. Could they have gone down a freight elevator? We'll see.

TSBD Entryway – 12:31

I was standing on the third step of the TSBD front entrance at 12:30:50.6, when AP photographer James Altgens snapped Altgens6, the photo (p. 111) that included the entrance of the TSBD in the background. Photography experts who have studied the picture for years have concluded that the area in and around the entryway was altered in several places, the top blacked out, but look at the man in the center of the left picture below.

Note the unbuttoned (hanging out) dark shirt with some sort of light pattern and long sleeves, also note the white V-neck T-shirt. This was a self-made V-neck because I had the habit of tugging down on the neck of my T-shirt with my fingers, stretching and deforming the neck. Now look at the other two images.

The WC said that wasn't me in the Altgens6 photo – that it was TSBD employee Billy Lovelady, *supposedly* standing on the *landing* of the entryway. Below are pictures of Billy, taken by the FBI, wearing the shirt he had on at noon on November 22, 1963. It has *short sleeves* with broad vertical *red and white stripes*, a white waistband, no missing buttons, and a white T-shirt with a rounded neck.

There are six stone steps below the landing of the TSBD entryway, and the figure standing beside the column is clearly on no higher than the third step from the bottom, not the landing on top. He's not high enough nor far back enough in the entryway to be up on the landing. And his shirt sure isn't striped. Billy also was 5'8", weighed 170 pounds, and was almost 27 years old. So, that's *not* Billy.

TSBD Entryway – 12:31

Detail of Commission Exhibit No. 369, Altgens6. The sun was shining directly into the entranceway at this moment. Why is it black? Arrow was drawn by Wesley Frazier during testimony.

How come the top part isn't all black, like in Altgens6?

About 1:00 to 1:15 P.M. Note that the men on upper steps – one on the landing exactly where Frazier had said he'd stood – are easily seen.

The headless man in a short-sleeved shirt (its stripes crudely whited out) with his elbows spread in Altgens6 (above) has to be Billy Lovelady. In front of the right shoulder of the headless man, there appears to be the upper right part of another man's head, with a large blob of whiteout obscuring the rest of the face. And who was that strange man to my left? There was no TSBD employee like that on the steps. This man with half a head was inserted into the photograph for some unknown reason. Bottom line: Altgens6 was substantially tampered with.

The handwritten notes of Detective Captain Will Fritz show that I told him I was "out with Bill Shelley in front," but in Algens6 Shelley's face was mostly whited out, Lovelady's head was blacked out, and on November 25 Truly said that the man beside the column in Altgens6 was Billy Lovelady. Another strike against Truly.

The images inserted to my left in Altgens6 distort my face and make it hard to perceive it clearly, so let's remove that bogus material and see what we find, below.

TSBD Entryway – 12:31

Guess what: it's me, Harvey – complete with my deep-set eyes, my nose, cheekbones, cleft chin, and customary pursed lips. Even my right ear matches. Some researchers think my hairline and forehead were altered, adding Lovelady's hairline and forehead, so let's remove those.

Altgens6

Does that look like Billy? Don't think so. For one thing, Billy's jaw – and entire face – are longer and narrower.

Billy   *Me*

Who would have made the alterations to Altgens6? Probably Jaggars-Chiles-Stovall, my former employer – located in Dallas, with the required photographic equipment and expertise, had worked for the CIA – now overseen by the FBI. One thing to keep in mind about the alterations: someone present at J-C-S had to have been familiar with my face, as well as those of Lovelady, Shelley, and Frazier. Some researchers also believe J-C-S was the field headquarters of the assassination.

Now read the WC testimony of Shelley, Lovelady, and others:

O. V. Campbell, FBI report: "...at about 12:30 P.M.... he and several other associates were together, stationed about 30 feet in front of this building facing away from the building....heard a loud report...believed the noise came from away from his building...observed the car bearing President Kennedy to slow down, a near stop...."

Roy Truly: "[I was standing with Mr. Campbell]...out in Elm Street, 10 to 15 or 20 feet from the front steps.... I think Bill Shelley was over to my right as I faced the motorcade...." Mrs. A. E. Reid also was with Truly, she said. Arnold and Rackley were by Campbell.

Harold Norman: Went outside with "Junior" Jarman, "I remember seeing Mr. Truly and Mr. Campbell. They were standing somewhere behind us, not exactly behind us but they were back of us." [Anybody else?] "Well, I believe Billy Lovelady, I think. He was sitting on the steps there." Shelley and Billy said Billy was sitting near the *top* of the steps, so why does Norman mention Billy? Norman and Jarman returned to the TSBD and went to the fifth floor before the motorcade arrived, Norman said.

Bill Shelley: "I went outside then to the front.... Several people were out there..., Lloyd Viles and Sarah Stanton.... *Wesley Frazier and Billy Lovelady joined us shortly afterwards."* [Standing where?] *"Just outside the glass doors."* [That would be on the top landing of the entrance?] *"Yes."*

In another statement Shelley said, "Lovelady was seated on the entrance steps in front of me.... Wesley Frazier, Mrs. Sarah Stanton and Mrs. Carolyn Arnold were also standing near me.... I did not see Lee Harvey Oswald." However, Arnold stated she was standing with Campbell, Viles said he was on the south side of Elm Street. Only Shelley put Frazier on the landing – no one else even mentioned seeing him.

Billy Lovelady: "[You ate your lunch on the steps?] "Yes, sir." [Who was with you?] "Bill Shelley and Sarah Stanton." [Where were you when the picture was taken? (Shown Altgens6 photograph.)] "Right there at the entrance of the building standing on the step, would be here." [You were standing on which step?] *"It would be your top level."* *[The top step, you were standing there?]* *"Right."*

In a May 24, 1964 *New York Herald-Tribune* article reported by Dom Bonafederted, "'*I was standing <u>on the first step,</u>*' [Lovelady] told me when I interviewed him.... 'Several people saw me. That lady shielding her eyes [bottom center of Altgens6 photo] works here on the second floor.'" Then Billy must have been the figure without a head standing right behind her. He ate his lunch at the top of the steps after he came out and then went down with Shelley to the bottom of the steps.

Sarah Stanton: "I was standing on the front steps with Mr. William Shelley, Mr. Otis Williams, Mrs. R. E. Sanders, and Billy Lovelady." She does not state when she stood there with them. She must have gone down with Shelley and Lovelady before Joe Molina came out. She was employed in the second floor office. She didn't testify for the WC, only gave a statement, which could have been edited and altered later, since it's quite short.

Mrs. R. E. (Pauline) Sanders: "I was standing on the top step at the east end...Sarah Stanton standing next to me." She, also, doesn't say *when* Stanton stood next to her, and since Molina and Williams were standing next to Sanders, Stanton must have gone down with Shelley and Lovelady.

Joe Molina: "At approximately 12:20 P.M....I left my office and took a position on the top step of the entrance of the Texas School Book Depository.... Otis Williams...and Mrs. Pauline Sanders were also viewing the motorcade with me." So, by about 12:20, Shelley, Lovelady and Stanton had gone down to the bottom of the steps. The entryway seems to be 12' wide at the top but only about 9' wide at the bottom. "I was right in the entrance." [Did you see a police officer with [Roy Truly]?] "I didn't see a police officer." He doesn't mention seeing Frazier at the top.

Otis Williams "I was standing on the top step against the railing on the east side of the steps.... I do not recall who was standing at either side of me," but he recalled Mrs. Sanders being up there. So, he stayed up at the top.

Mrs. Avery Davis: "At about 12:15...I took up a position on one of the lower steps of the building entrance. Judy McCully...was standing by me, at my left."

So, Shelley was standing near Campbell, out toward the Elm Street curb, and at the same time he was on the top step next to Lovelady. And Lovelady was standing on the landing, while sitting one step below and also standing near Truly, beside Shelley. And Wesley Frazier came out with Shelley and Lovelady and stood on the landing, along with

Lloyd Viles and Sarah Stanton. But only Billy himself actually puts himself on the landing – and *not one of the people above* puts Billy next to the column, where I was standing, *except Billy*, who places himself in two different locations at the same time, when he *actually* was at a third location. Any questions?

Now, *all* employees working in the TSBD on November 22 gave statements, which included where each person was when the shots were fired. *Not one* of the male employees put himself on the bottom steps of the entranceway. Then who – unless Lovelady and Shelley – were the headless man and the faceless man on the bottom steps? And what about the man with the tie missing the top of his head, the fantastic half head of a black guy in profile coming out of the pillar over my stomach, and the woman with added hair to my left?

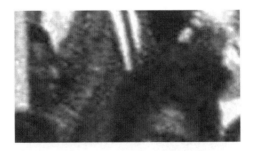

But wait, we haven't heard from Wesley Frazier, the

WC's star witness – the patsy used by the plotters to help frame a patsy, me. When Frazier testified for the WC, he and the WC lawyer did a lot of dancing around – I think it was a jittery jitterbug – so stay with me:

"I was standing on the steps...pretty close to Mr. Shelley and this boy Billy Lovelady...[and a] lady...whose name is Sarah.... I was...one step down from the top there...standing there by the rail.... [At the sound of the shots I] stood right where I was." [And Mr. Shelley was still standing there?] "Right." [And also Billy Lovelady?] "Yes, sir...." Why is the WC attorney asking *only* about Shelley and Lovelady up there? Must be because they were at the bottom – but, how dumb, trying to put Billy near the top, when he *supposedly* was by the column – where, actually, *I* was standing.

"[You see anybody after that come into the building?] "Somebody other, that didn't work there?" [A police officer.] "No, sir...." [...No police officer came up the steps and into the building?] "Not that I know." How could Wesley not see motorcycle cop Marrion L. Baker, who said he charged into the building less than half a minute after the shots? And Joe Molina said he didn't see Baker come in either. Neither Shelley nor Lovelady, nor anyone else on the steps, mentioned seeing Baker. And why did the WC attorney even ask that question? The first discordant note struck in what would be the Baker symphony of fairy tales.

"[Did [the police] ask you where you had been?] "I told them I was out on the steps there." [And who you were with?] "I told them, and naturally Mr. Shelley and Billy vouched for me...." Naturally. And he vouched for them. Naturally.

"[When you stood out on the front..., where was Shelley standing and where was Lovelady standing...?] "Well, see, I was standing, like I say, one step down from the top, and Mr. Shelley was standing, you know, back from the top step and over toward the side of the wall there. See, he was standing right over there, and then Billy was a couple of steps down from me over toward the wall also.... Billy, like I say, is two or three steps down in front of me." [Do you recognize this fellow?] "That is Billy, that is Billy Lovelady...." [Let's take a marker and make an *arrow* down that way. That mark is Billy Lovelady?] "Right." [(He was) in front of you to the right over to the wall?] "Yes." [The arrow marks 'Billy Lovelady' on the Commission's Exhibit No. 369.]" Notice all the dancing around about Lovelady and Shelley.

TSBD Entryway – 12:31

Five years later, February 13, 1969, at the New Orleans Clay Shaw trial – new town, new D.A., a courtroom, no FBI agents feeding lines – Wesley forgot the most crucial part of his script, since he wasn't a *professional* liar. [...Recall who you were with...?] "When I was standing there at the top of the stairs I was...by a heavyset lady...her name is Sarah...." [Anyone else...?] "<u>Right down in front of me at the bottom of the steps</u> my foreman Bill Shelley and Billy Lovelady were standing there." Again, Wesley doesn't say *when Sarah* was up there.

[...Where did you go after....] "I didn't go anywhere. I just stayed right where I was." [Did you ever see Lee Harvey Oswald during that time that you were on the steps....?] "No, sir, I did not." If he *did* stay right where he was, that may account for the top part of the entryway in Altgens6 being completely blacked out, since Shelley and Lovelady would have been seen missing but Frazier still there. Or...could have shown Frazier missing too.

Game, set, match. Wesley didn't ever see me, *he says*, but <u>Lovelady and Shelley were at the bottom of the steps</u> – right by me, with Shelley almost completely deleted from Altgens6, Lovelady's head obviously blacked out and his striped shirt obviously whited out. Based on the testimonies

133

above, the people on the landing – *from east to west* – were Sanders, Molina, Williams, and maybe Frazier. Down four or five steps – *from west to east* – were me beside the column, Shelley and Lovelady, with Mrs. Avery Davis and Judy McCully to their left, Sarah Stanton below Billy, her right hand shading her eyes. Since office workers didn't interact with warehouse workers, Stanton, Williams, Molina, Sanders, Davis, and McCully didn't know me.

So, after fifty-two years, we finally know: if Frazier was standing on top just west of the handrail, that would have put him directly above Lovelady and Shelley, who were near the bottom of the steps. Lovelady was standing to Shelley's left, arms and hands raised to shield his eyes from the sun, Shelley was to Billy's right, and I was next to the column, to Shelley's right, just as I told Dallas Detective Captain Will Fritz. When I came out of the building, shortly before 12:25, *if* Frazier was still at the top of the steps, I would have walked past his right, so he'd have had to have seen me go down the steps, and Shelley, of course, also saw me, when I arrived next to him at the bottom.

Frazier told other versions of his story in later testimony and interviews, and – in proper CIA form, like

Shelley and Lovelady – tried to keep his statements narrowed, not saying *when* he was at the top of the steps, so at 12:30 he could've been at the top, or at the bottom. In either case, he, like Shelley and Lovelady, knew that I'd been on the steps by the column. The top of the entryway above me was blacked out in Altgens6 to hide the fact that *Shelley and Lovelady weren't up on the landing, but near the bottom of the steps.* Frazier might not have been up on the landing, either.

It's sad that Lovelady and Frazier said nothing about where I was when the shots rang out, but I guess they thought their lives were in danger if they didn't toe the line, and who cares about defaming a dead "commie defector" anyway – not to mention creating a legacy for my two daughters, wife and friends that I was an assassin and traitor. Still, a lot of witnesses like these two guys *were* murdered. And Wesley Frazier was terrorized, as we'll see.

But let's be clear about at least one thing: if I *was* in the TSBD entryway, then all discussions about 'my' rifle, its purchase, its ownership, its condition, its rate of fire, its accuracy, its ammunition, its shell casings, number of shots fired, and where it was found are academic. I wasn't at that sixth floor window shooting at anyone – and that rifle was a plant, conceivably even put there by Truly, or Shelley.

Escape & The Witnesses

Almost immediately after the flurry of shots rang out over Elm Street, Vickie Adams and Sandra Styles ran from their fourth floor window perch to the rear of the building and down the northwest stairs, arriving at the first floor about a minute later, or around 12:32, Vickie testified, and ran out a back door. The WC later *inserted into Vickie's sworn testimony*, "...and encountered Bill Shelley and Bill Lovelady on the first floor," in an attempt to create a more favorable time line for their claim that I was "a lone nut" – but Vickie always denied that the two men were there, as did Sandra.

Bill Shelley testified that immediately after the shots "... Billy Lovelady and myself took off across the street to that little old island.... Officers started running down to the railroad yards, and Billy and I walked down that way." They didn't come back into the building for about five minutes, they testified.

However, previously, on November 22, 1963, Shelley

gave an affidavit, in which he stated, "I heard what sounded like three shots.... I ran across the street to the corner of the park & ran into a girl [Gloria Calvery] crying & she said the President had been shot. I went back to the building & went back inside & called my wife & told her what happened. I was on the first floor then & I stayed at the [southeast?] elevator & was told [by Roy Truly] not to let anyone out of the elevator. I left the elevator and went with the police on up to the other floors. I left Jack Dougherty in charge of the elevator." No mention of Billy Lovelady, the jaunt to the rail yards, or coming back through a side door five minutes later. Nor seeing Vickie Adams.

The WC also substituted "Truly" for "Shelley" late in Vickie's transcript, apparently trying to get Truly to the rear of the first floor, although Vickie had earlier testified that *she never saw Truly*, and Truly didn't see Vickie. Vickie told researcher Barry Ernest that testimony in her transcript had been falsified.

Motorcycle cop Marion L. Baker testified before the WC on March 25, 1964 – *so he and Truly had had four months after the assassination to polish up their story*. As you read Baker's 'let's pretend' account, remember that I was standing on the TSBD steps the whole time.

Baker said that he was riding his bike north on Houston Street, 60 feet past Main Street, beside the 4th press car. Seeing a flock of pigeons fly up from the TSBD roof at the first shot, he came roaring down the street, a distance of 180 to 200 feet. He jumped off his bike approximately 45 feet from the doorway of the TSBD, he said, pushed his way through the crowd of people standing outside, and rushed by me into the building, although Frazier and Molina, at the top of the stairs, testified they didn't see him come by them.

Truly saw Baker, ran after him – right past me – into the lobby, told Baker he was the building manager, and the two of them ran to the freight elevators near the northwest corner, they testified – a distance of 80-110 feet. Truly did *not* see Shelley and Lovelady there. Both elevators were stuck on the fifth floor, they testified, so Truly rushed up the stairs. Baker followed him, gun drawn.

A *big* problem with the Baker/Truly story is that if it happened as told they would have reached the stairs about fifty seconds after the first shot, but Vickie Adams and Saundra Styles were still coming down the stairs at that time – and Vickie later told researcher Barry Ernest that she didn't see Truly, Baker, Shelley, Lovelady or Lee Oswald

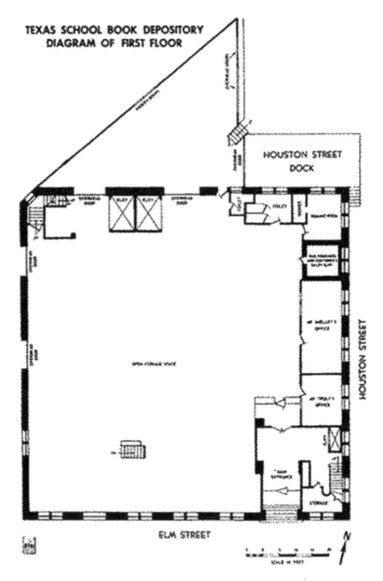

Commission Exhibit No. 1061

on her way down and out of the building. Keep in mind that Vickie had nothing at stake – Truly may very well have.

Also note Baker's immediate recognition of a rifle shot and instantaneous reaction to it, in contrast to virtually everyone else in Dealey Plaza. Most people, including sheriff's deputies, policemen and Secret Service men – many of them combat veterans or long-time hunters – either didn't realize that the first shot was a rifle report or didn't respond to it. So, was the entire Truly/Baker account fabricated? Let's hear the rest, anyway – the WC testimony and Lee's *theoretical* descent from the sixth floor to the lunchroom *in this supposed scenario*.

When Lee got down to the fifth floor, right after the shooting, he must've heard the heels of Vickie and Sandra rushing down the stairs from the fourth floor, so he paused for thirty seconds until the echoing sound of their heels faded, then continued hurrying down himself. It had slowed him, but he didn't want them to hear him. He reached the second floor, when the footsteps of Truly and Baker came pounding up the stairs. Lee quickly walked toward the lunchroom, pulled open the door and went inside, just as Truly and Baker said they charged onto the second floor.

Lee had arrived too late – Baker had come too quickly. His motorcycle and foot dash was later timed by the WC at ninety seconds, making his supposed confrontation with

Lee begin at about 12:32:20. However, it could have been fifteen or twenty seconds later, since on November 22 Baker was pushing his way through a crowd of people on the sidewalk and entryway stairs, which would have slowed him down, as Baker admitted. In addition, although Baker said it took him fifteen seconds to get to the TSBD, later investigations showed it was probably twenty-two seconds. So, it could have taken Lee as much as a minute and fifty-seven seconds to get into the lunchroom, or 12:32:44.

Truly took two or three steps up toward the third floor, he said, realized Baker wasn't following him and returned to the landing. He heard a voice from the lunchroom and "saw the officer almost directly in the doorway of the lunchroom facing Lee Harvey Oswald."

Baker swore in a November 22, 1963 affidavit, "I saw a man walking away from the stairway. I called to the man, and he turned around and came back toward me.... [He]... was *a white man, approximately 30 years old, 5'9", 165 pounds, dark hair*, and wearing a light brown jacket.... The manager said, 'I know that man; he works here.'"

The weight, hair color and age were that of *Lee Oswald*. The pictures of Lee in the Marines show him looking five to six years older than his age even then (p. 19). But how

Escape & The Witnesses

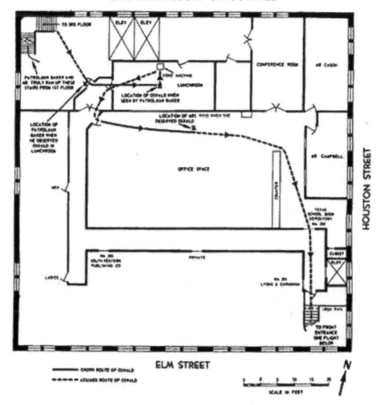

could Truly have mistaken Lee for me? Truly knew me, had hired me, saw me every day. Lee was thirty pounds heavier, had dark hair that receded like a widow's peak, was two inches taller, and looked six years older than me.

I'd told employee Eddie Piper at 12:00 that I was *going up* to eat, and Carolyn Arnold saw me eating in the second floor lunchroom at 12:15. Plus – something most people aren't aware of – JFK's motorcade was five minutes late. He had been scheduled to pass the TSBD at 12:25. Why would I be eating in the lunchroom at 12:15 if I intended to shoot JFK at 12:25, and then be in the lunchroom again at 12:32 – *supposedly* now wearing a jacket – and walking *away* from the lunchroom door?

Since everyone before and after Baker's encounter said Lee was wearing just a white T-shirt, where did the "light brown jacket" come from? Baker didn't submit his affidavit until late afternoon or early evening of November 22, by which time the "official line" was that "Lee Harvey Oswald" had killed Officer Tippit, wearing a light-colored jacket found two-and-a-half blocks from the murder scene. It was crucial to tie me to the Tippit murder, so it seems that Baker's report followed the "official line."

Baker testified for the WC, "I caught a glimpse of him and I ran over there and opened that door and hollered at him.... He was walking away from me, about 20 feet away from me in the lunchroom...walking east." [...he then walked back toward you?] "Yes, sir." [...anything in his hands?] "He had nothing at that time. [Was he calm and collected?] "Yes, sir. He never did say a word or nothing.

In fact, he didn't change his expression one bit.... As I left, he was still in the position that he was...."

Baker also was asked, "Do you recall whether or not [Oswald] was wearing the same clothes...in the police station as when you saw him in the lunchroom," and he responded, "Actually, just looking at him, he looked like he didn't have the same thing on." But the WC attorney didn't ask Baker *what* the difference in clothing was.

Truly and Baker testified that they resumed running up the stairs until they got to *the fifth floor*, from where they took the east elevator to the seventh floor. Why try an elevator? And why the *east* elevator? The *west* elevator was closer to the stairs. Truly and Baker then "ran up a little stairway that leads out through a little penthouse on to the roof."

Baker said he looked around the roof for several minutes, checking out "some kind of a shack on the northeast corner," but found nothing, so they went back downstairs, they testified. This is the tale Baker and Truly told the Warren Commission.

Employee James" Junior" Jarman had been watching the motorcade on *the fifth floor* with two friends. What he testified to the WC helps give the lie to the Truly/Baker WC testimony: "[How long was it before you ran to the west end [of the building] from the time of the shots...?]" "After the third shot was fired, I would say it was about a minute...." [And where did you go then?] "We ran to the elevator, *but the elevator had gone down*...." [Which elevator did you run to?] "The elevator on the west side." [On the west. That [elevator] wasn't there?] "No, sir."

At that time, Truly and Baker were supposedly running up the stairs, and the two elevators were supposedly stuck on the fifth floor. Jarman says nothing about the east elevator. The WC attorney doesn't ask. Jarman and his two friends then *ran down the stairs*. Jarman does *not* say that he met Truly and Baker coming up the stairs. The WC attorney doesn't ask.

Before trying further to figure out how all this really went down, let's look at another part of Baker's November 22 *sworn* affidavit:

"I was riding motorcycle escort for the President.... <u>Just as I approached Elm Street and Houston I heard three shots</u>. I realized those shots were rifle shots *and <u>I began to try to figure out</u>* where they came from. I decided the shots had come from the building on the

146

northwest corner of Elm and Houston.... I jumped off my motor and ran inside the building." Note that he didn't instantaneously roar down Houston Street on his bike for 180-200 feet.

"As I entered the door...*I saw several people standing around.* I asked [them] where the stairs were. *A man stepped forward and stated he was the building manager* and that he would show me where the stairs were. I followed the man to the rear of the building, [but] ...the elevator was hung several floors up so we used the stairs instead. As we reached <u>the third or fourth floor</u> I saw a man walking away from the stairway. I called to the man and...the manager said, 'I know that man, he works here.' I then turned the man loose and went up to the top floor...."

According to FBI affidavits by TSBD employees, no man was on the third or fourth floors then. Notice there is no mention of an encounter with "Oswald" on the first floor, no mention of an encounter in the second floor lunchroom. No mention of pigeons. People "standing around" inside? There were none then. A sworn affidavit by a Dallas police officer. The WC swept all of this under its rug.

Now consider that <u>the entire</u> Truly/Baker story (both versions) is fiction. There was a report that Truly and Baker had stopped "Oswald" *on the first floor*, and that Truly had identified "Oswald" as an employee. The only "Oswald" inside the TSBD at that moment was Lee, on the first floor, so both the WC lunchroom story spun by Truly/Baker and Baker's affidavit must now be called into question. If in fact Truly and Baker remained on the first floor, that would have allowed the time and space for the three assassins still upstairs to be escorted down a freight elevator by a TSBD employee conspirator.

But let's follow Lee, whether he met Baker on the second floor or not. He bought a Coke from the machine in the lunchroom, removed its cap, and then sauntered into the north entrance of the second floor offices, just as Mrs. Reid entered the south entrance, about 12:33. She testified:

"I looked up and Oswald was coming in the back door of the office.... *He had on a white T-shirt* and some kind of wash trousers.... *He did not have any jacket on*.... He had gotten a Coke and was holding it in his right hand.... I met him...and I said, "Oh, the President has been shot, but maybe they didn't hit him." He mumbled something to me, I kept walking, he did, too...he was very calm. *I thought it was a little strange that one of the warehouse boys would be up in the office....* The only time I had seen him in the office was to come and get change." Asked by the WC how many times she'd seen Oswald since he began working there, she said about five times: "I can't recall seeing him [in the lunchroom] but three times." So she wasn't very familiar with my face and build, like Truly was.

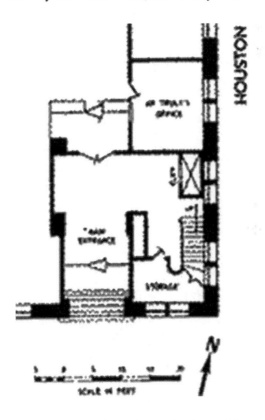

Lee continued walking through the office and went down the southeast stairs to the first floor. He ducked into a small storage room beside the steps to put down his Coke bottle. TSBD Vice President O. V. Campbell was then running into the building. He turned right, toward the southeast passenger elevator and stairs, heading for his second floor office. He had just missed running into Lee coming down the stairs.

The next day Campbell was quoted by the *New York Herald Tribune* as saying, "Shortly after the shooting, we raced back into the building.... We saw him (Oswald) in a small storage room on the first floor. Then we noticed he was gone." Who was "we"? And being Vice President of TSBD, Campbell had seen very little of me, so, like all other witnesses, he thought Lee was me.

Reporter Kent Biffle of *The Dallas Morning News* overheard Truly telling Captain Will Fritz that he had seen "Oswald" near the [southeast] storage room, which raises the question of *when* Truly reputedly saw "Oswald." Published on November 23, Biffle wrote that, "In a storage room on the first floor, the officer [Marrion Baker], gun drawn, spotted Oswald. 'Does this man work here?' the officer reportedly asked Truly." Truly said he did. Notice that – as in the lunchroom tale – it's again Truly who 'saves' Lee from capture.

The story was corroborated several times. The *Sydney Morning Herald* (11/23/63) reported that "Oswald…was stopped by a policeman. Oswald told the policeman that, 'I work here,' and when another employee confirmed that he did, *the policeman let Oswald walk away*." Detective Ed Hicks told the *London Free Press* (11/23/63) that *as Oswald came out* "a policeman asked him where he was going. He said he wanted to see what the excitement was all about." James Jarman told the HSCA, "I heard that Oswald had come down through the [second floor] office and came down the front stairs, and he was stopped by the officer….and Mr. Truly told them that was alright, that he worked here, so *then [Lee Oswald] proceeded on out of the building…*," to be met outside by NBC White House correspondent Robert MacNeil (p. 161).

This account seems to be the "smoking gun" that shoots down the Truly/Baker lunchroom testimony, but raises another question: why did either Truly or Baker even notice Lee – and, considering Lee's timeline, the event had to have been just after 12:33. That being so, what had Truly and Baker been doing for the previous two minutes? And what did they do after they encountered Lee? According to Dorothy Ann Garner, Vickie Adams' supervisor, she saw a policeman come up the stairs to the fourth floor, *after*

Vickie and Sandra had gone down. So, the lunchroom encounter did not take place but perhaps Truly/Baker's climb up the stairs (exactly when?) *might* have.

Let's consider one final possibility. Suppose that not only the new U.S. President, the FBI director and his agents, CIA officials, Chief Justice of the Supreme Court, generals and doctors helped to cover up the conspiracy but also Dallas policemen. By the time this story is told, you'll see that at least ten to fifteen Dallas police of all ranks participated in my frame up and/or the coverup, so let's examine the possibility that Officer Baker was one of these.

What if Baker's mad dash into the TSBD was not to try to catch a rooftop sniper but to help – with Truly – the assassins in the TSBD to escape? *Or*, had Baker also been ordered there to kill "Oswald," and Truly stopped Baker by the storage room only when he saw that the "Oswald" standing there was Lee, not me? Killing "Oswald" just then – 'resisting arrest' – would have wrapped up the JFK murder, closing the case in five minutes, as the plotters hoped.

Accounts of *all* TSBD employees show that *everyone* was either outside, on the steps, or looking out of south-facing windows overlooking Elm Street. Only Vickie and

Sandra were immediately in motion after the shots, and they were gone from the building in just over a minute – *never having seen Truly and Baker*. And *the only policeman* to rush into the TSBD immediately was Baker. All the rest were running to the "grassy knoll."

That opens up a new possible scenario: A TSBD conspirator on the sixth floor – for instance, Jack Dougherty had no alibi, was considered suspicious by a WC attorney, and testified he went to the sixth floor at 12:30 – takes the three assassins down on the east freight elevator to the first floor at around 12:32, then goes back up to the fifth floor – making sure that the west freight elevator has its gate up so it can't be called down, while Truly and Baker are near the front doors to prevent anyone from coming to the rear of the first floor. No TSBD employee was then at the rear of the first floor.

Since Truly/Baker don't charge up the stairs to encounter Lee, Lee has time to wait for Vickie and Sandra to reach the first floor and exit the building, after which Lee goes down, gets a Coke, is met by Mrs. Reid at 12:33, giving him over two minutes to get there from the sixth floor corner *southwest* windows, continues to the first floor and is seen by Truly, Baker and Campbell in, or by, the small storage room.

The other three assassins run out the back door, watched over by a policeman Vickie Adams sees on the east side of the TSBD (p. 164). A witness – *not* called by the WC – later testified at the New Orleans Clay Shaw trial that immediately after the shooting three men ran from behind the TSBD, two jumped into a parked car on Houston and roared away (p. 167). That scenario answers a lot of questions.

But why did Truly and Baker say they had encountered "Lee Harvey Oswald" in the second floor lunchroom, when I was out front on the steps and Lee was on the first floor in the small storage room? Simple: the plotters didn't want the

Sixth floor.

"lone nut" to be seen downstairs less than three minutes after the shooting, especially since Vickie and Sandra hadn't heard Lee come down. The *supposed* timeline of "Oswald" going from the sixth floor *southeast* corner "sniper's nest" to the second floor lunchroom was tenuous enough – the sixth floor was filled with tall stacks of boxes full of books.

Sixth floor.

"Oswald" being in the first floor storage room so soon must have seemed untenable to those orchestrating the frame up, so Truly and Baker were told to report "Oswald" in the second floor lunchroom, creating a more believable time line. That's also why the transcript of Vickie's testimony was altered.

In addition, the Truly/Baker lunchroom story precludes the possibility of other shooters, since the elevators were said to be stuck on the fifth floor, so no assassins could have taken one of those down – and since Truly and Baker supposedly were charging up the steps, no one could have come down the steps, either. Which left only "the lone nut" in the lunchroom. Clever tale. Nice try. Never happened. I was out on the front steps. Need to move on now.

I was told by my control to be at lunch on the second floor lunchroom, so that people would see me there, then if someone later saw Lee there, they would think it was me, which is what happened when Mrs. Reid saw him. Next, I had to be in the crowd outside after 12:20, so that there was no chance of two 'Lee Harvey Oswalds' being seen inside the TSBD after 12:25, and I needed to leave soon after the shooting, so that 'Lee Harvey Oswald' could exit the TSBD without arousing suspicion, otherwise my 'twin' would have walked right by me. That wouldn't do.

The plotters were relying on the chaos of the assassination scene to create confusion about where "Oswald" really was, and if anyone saw Lee Oswald, they'd think it was me, Harvey. Shakespeare would have loved it: a tragedy wrapped in a comedy – doubles walking out the same door within a minute of each other, fake policemen, fake Secret Service men. And it was all written and directed by the CIA's playwright David Atlee Phillips, master illusionist, who certainly had read Shakespeare.

A lot of questions remain about the TSBD's role in all this – mainly, how did four assassins and three rifles (two good rifles and 'my' rifle) get into the TSBD, plus if someone opened the entrance to the roof so they could enter, who was it? And it's likely that one evening after work, before November 22, the assassins had been given a guided tour of the TSBD, so they'd know where to run, where to hide, where to enter and exit. They even could have stored their rifles on the seventh floor the night of November 21. David Atlee Phillips may have been there to choreograph the scenario. So, who helped them someone associated with building owner Byrd, or Truly, or Shelley?

My money is on Bill Shelley. Here's why: William Weston has written: "On October 29, 1945, Hugh Perry hired a mysterious clerk named William Hoyt Shelley [to work at the TSBD]. According to news journalist Elzie [Dean] Glaze, who met him in 1974, Shelley said he was an intelligence agent during the war [WWII] and afterwards joined the CIA." If Shelley was hired by the TSBD in 1945, how could he have been working for the CIA later? The CIA wasn't created until 1947, so this implies that Shelley was CIA while working for the TSBD – and suggests that the TSBD may have been CIA affiliated, in 1963 involved with some anti-Castro activities. Researchers Ralph Cinque and Jim Fetzer have written, "…Shelley was a career CIA agent, and we have reasons to believe he was deeply involved in the [JFK] plot."

And why did Shelley pull his crew from the sixth floor for lunch "around" 11:50 – two crew members testified it was 11:45. Regular lunch break was 12:00 to 12:45, the crew usually went down at 11:55. Was going down at 11:45 done to give the shooters in the TSBD an extra ten minutes to prepare? Lovelady testified, "Mr. Shelley would come up every once in a while, check on us. He wasn't workin' with us but he would come up see how we gettin' along." So Shelley must have come up to lead the crew down for lunch.

There also is a published report that soon after the assassination Shelley was arrested and formally charged with the murder of JFK. Why? He was taken to the DPD Headquarters at 1:30 P.M., was not allowed to leave until 5:00 P.M. and was required to submit a second statement. He most likely was released when the DPD heard from the CIA that Shelley was one of theirs.

Although Shelley may well have helped the assassins bring their rifles into the TSBD and unlocked the door to the roof, it also could have been the *Acme Building and Maintenance Company* (ABMC). Every weekday night, two ABMC cleaners with a key to the building came in after business hours and worked in the TSBD until midnight. They could have let the assassins in and opened the roof door; the rifles could have been put in the seventh floor store room. Yet no one working for ABMC was ever interviewed by the Dallas Police or the FBI, and the WC never mentioned ABMC in its report.

Like TSBD, ABMC had some mystery shrouding it. Founded by Frank T. Jones, ABMC was one of the leading cleaning companies in Dallas. Early in 1964 it was sold to ARA Building Services – *a company formed in the summer of 1963* – and ABMC was quickly absorbed into ARA. Although ABMC had been in business for over forty years, the office of the Texas Secretary of State later claimed the company had never existed – nor did the Dallas Chamber of Commerce know of the company. ARA was bought out in 1969. ABMC owner Frank T. Jones was a member of the Dallas Citizens Council, which put together the luncheon for JFK at the Dallas Trade Mart on November 22. Jones obviously knew Truly.

In any case, I was still outside the TSBD, in my rust-brown tweed shirt, just after 12:32 P.M., when a guy about 29 years old ran up and asked for a phone. I knew where that phone was. I pointed to the lobby and said, "It's in there." We made brief eye contact, and then he ran in. The man was Pierce M. Allman, who was then a program director for the Dallas television and radio station WFAA. He needed a phone to call his station, talked on that pay phone for the next forty minutes, describing what was taking place on the first floor of the TSBD. *The Dallas Morning News* reporter Kent Biffle saw him there.

Across Houston Street from the TSBD, while waiting for the motorcade and looking down from the window of a sewing room, Mrs. Louis Velez and two co-workers had seen Jack Ruby walking up and down the street by the TSBD. These women probably were employees of McKell's Sportswear, a women's clothing manufacturer in the Dal-Tex Building, 501 Elm Street (see next page).

KRLD-TV reporter and future Dallas mayor Wes Wise saw Jack Ruby walking around the corner of the TSBD a few minutes after the assassination. Some believe that the man with the hat to my right in Altgens6 is Jack Ruby.

After the shots rained down on Elm Street, I knew I had to leave and get instructions from an intelligence contact at the Texas Theatre, as I'd been instructed. I turned left

Altgens6 detail. Dal-Tex Building, northeast corner of Houston and Elm, across the street from the TSBD entryway. At upper right may have been the women who saw Ruby and Lee Oswald. They certainly had direct line of sight. Note the man sitting on the fire escape. Why is his jacket on the railing?

and began to walk east on Elm Street. Less than a minute later, NBC White House correspondent Robert MacNeil ran toward the TSBD, looking for a phone:

"As I ran up the steps and through the door, a young man in shirt sleeves was coming out. In great agitation I asked him where there was a phone. He pointed inside to an open space where another man was talking on the phone situated near a column and said, 'Better ask him.' I [went] inside and asked the second man [Pierce Allman], who pointed to an office at one side. I found a telephone on the desk [there].... My New York news desk has since placed the time of my call at 12:36."

The young man MacNeil spoke with had to have been Lee. Who else would be *leaving* the TSBD *at 12:34 and not know where a phone might be inside*? Employees were not leaving – they were rushing into the building. And the only young white males working in the TSBD that day were Lovelady, Frazier and me.

When Lee exited the TSBD and came down the steps, Mrs. Velez and her two friends saw Ruby give Lee a handgun. The women supposedly said they knew "Lee Harvey Oswald," *who spoke Spanish very well* and who they'd eaten with at a nearby restaurant – remember that the Carrousel Club was only eight blocks southeast of the TSBD. Two of the women were said to be acquainted with Jack Ruby. The women were never interviewed by the FBI.

Lee then walked a short distance west on the Elm Street extension in front of the TSBD and waited. At 12:40 – the same time as I was getting on a bus down Elm Street – a light green Nash Rambler station wagon with a chrome luggage rack and an out-of-state license plate came slowly west on Elm Street, pulled over to the curb and stopped opposite the TSBD.

Dallas Deputy Sheriff Roger Craig, on the south side of Elm Street, heard a shrill whistle and saw a young man wearing a white T-shirt run to the car and get in. Craig later identified him as "Lee Harvey Oswald." The driver of the station wagon was a husky-looking Latin, with dark wavy hair, *wearing a tan windbreaker jacket.*

Two men in cars behind the Rambler also observed Lee entering the car. Witness Helen Forrest saw the same man run to the Rambler and get in. She said, "If it wasn't Oswald, it was his identical twin." The Rambler then drove west under the triple overpass, heading toward Oak Cliff.

A few minutes later the Rambler must have turned left at the Gloco gas station (next page), 1502 North Zangs, on the southwest corner of the intersection (which was about 1.5 miles from the TSBD), probably passing Officer J. D. Tippit parked in his patrol car at Gloco, and drove south on Lancaster Avenue toward East 10th Street. What happened then? In the next few minutes Lee obviously got a jacket from someone – maybe the driver of the Rambler.

Meanwhile, around 12:32, Vickie Adams and Sandra Styles had rushed out a back door to the Houston Street dock and down some steps towards the rear of the dock. Vickie continued, "At the time I left the building on the

Probable route (shaded) of Rambler and Lee to Oak Cliff.

Houston Street dock, there was an officer standing about two yards from the curb...and when we were running [from] the dock...he didn't encounter us or ask us what we were doing or where we were going."

So, a curiosity: what was that cop by the east side of the

TSBD doing there? Most policemen were running toward the "grassy knoll" at that moment. Could he have been waiting for the killers to come out a back door? And if anyone had challenged them, would he have vouched for them and said they were Secret Service agents? There were two phony cops on the "grassy knoll." Was this another one? And witnesses *had* seen one man in a suit at the sixth floor southwest windows and a man in a sport coat at the southeast windows.

Then Vickie and Sandra "went west towards the tracks…approximately two yards within the tracks, and there was an officer standing there, and he said, 'Get back to the building.'" Again, was he a real cop, another phony cop, or a cop helping with the cover-up? Easy to get paranoid about this.

Vickie and Sandra started back but went south and east down the Elm street extension in front of the TSBD. Sandra went inside, and later stated she "took the elevator to the fourth floor," while Vickie continued to look around outside. She testified she noticed a man, whom she later saw on television, Jack Ruby, standing on the corner of Houston and Elm shortly before she went back into the

TSBD, around 12:36. He must have been waiting there to give Lee the handgun.

Vickie finally went inside, pushed the button for the southeast passenger elevator, but the power was off, so she went up the nearby stairs to the second floor and walked across the building to the freight elevators. "I went into the [west] elevator which was stopped on the second floor, with two men who were dressed in suits and hats, and I assumed they were plainclothesmen." Then she "tried to get the elevator to go to the fourth floor, but it wasn't operating, so the gentlemen lifted the elevator gate and we went out...."

Wait a minute: two strange men in suits and hats are standing in a motionless elevator on the second floor? So, who were they, why were they on the elevator, where did they come from, and *where did they go*? This was only 5-6 minutes after the shooting – how could two plainclothesmen have arrived there so soon? And just standing still on a powerless elevator on the second floor?

But the WC didn't ask Vickie a single question about these men! The WC had pinpointed where every TSBD employee was in and around the building, but wasn't interested in two strange men standing motionless on an elevator car that had no power at 12:36?! And all TSBD employee affidavits state that no one saw any strange men in the TSBD that day.

Plus, why did the east elevator *supposedly* work for Truly and Baker, the passenger elevator worked for Sandra Styles, but the passenger elevator and west elevator didn't work for Vickie? And who had brought the west elevator down to the second floor? No one ever bothered to ask.

Witness James Worrell saw a man in a sport coat run out of the back of the TSBD. Witnesses had seen a man in a sport coat with a rifle in the sixth floor southeast window of the TSBD before the shooting. Worrell also testified he heard four shots, saw the front of the rifle above him, and that the barrel only extended four-inches from its stock, like a Mauser.

Another witness, Richard Randolph Carr, who the WC never saw fit to call, testified at the New Orleans Clay Shaw trial in 1969 that he was on the seventh floor of the New Courthouse Building, then under construction, at Houston and Commerce Streets (two blocks south of Elm), facing Dealey Plaza. He saw a Rambler station wagon parked on the wrong side of Houston, facing north, next to the TSBD.

He stated, "Immediately after the shooting there was three men that emerged from behind [the northeast corner of] the School Book Depository. There was a Latin – I can't say whether he was Spanish, Cuban, but he was real dark-complected – stepped out and opened the door; two men entered that station wagon; and the Latin drove it north on Houston. The car was in motion before the rear door was closed."

The third man, whom Carr said he'd seen in a TSBD window earlier, crossed to the east side of Houston, walked south "in a very big hurry – every once in a while he would look over his shoulder, as if he was being followed...." Then he turned left on Commerce Street, heading toward town. "He had on a felt hat, a light hat, he had on heavy-rimmed glasses, dark, heavy ear pieces on his glasses...[and] he had on a tie, ...a light shirt, a tan sport coat."

Asked by District Attorney Jim Garrison if he'd spoken to FBI agents about this incident, Carr said, "Yes, I did." What did they tell him to do, Garrison asked. "I done as I was instructed – I shut my mouth," Carr replied.

To And From 1026

After I left the TSBD I walked five blocks east on Elm Street (about .4 of a mile), when I saw a "Marsalis" bus stopped in traffic. "He come up and beat on the door of the bus…about even with Griffin Street," bus driver Cecil J. McWatters later testified. He let me on, I paid my fare and went to sit on the second cross seat on the right. It was 12:40, bus driver McWatters firmly testified.

Although I didn't notice her, my former landlady, Mrs.

Mary Bledsoe, was sitting at the front of the bus, opposite the driver. She testified to the WC that I had on "a brown shirt....hole in his sleeve, right elbow...all the buttons torn off.... Shirt open...tucked in.... Pants...were gray, and they were all ragged...at the waist." Mrs. Bledsoe was shown the shirt I had on when I was arrested (p.98), and she insisted that it was the shirt I was wearing on the bus. The WC counsel bent over backwards trying to make her say it was another brown shirt, but she stuck to her identification: "That is it.... Yes, it is the shirt." *So I didn't change my shirt when I got to my room!* She didn't identify either of the two pairs of pants that the WC counsel showed her.

At 12:45 the description of a suspect was broadcast over the police radio. Notice how it matches Baker's report: "White male, approximately 30, 165 pounds, slender build...." Did the dispatcher get that from Baker, or did Baker get that description from the broadcast? And Baker saw me later that day at the police station – how could he think I weighed 165 pounds and looked 30 years old?

People were pointing fingers at me within fifteen minutes of the shooting. The very first phone call the police got was from an anonymous Bell Helicopter employee, who suggested, "Oswald did it." I had no friends or acquaintances in Dallas, and the only person I knew who worked at Bell was Michael Paine. And guess who quickly alerted Police Captain Will Fritz to the fact that I was gone from the TSBD? My good friend Roy S. Truly.

Meanwhile, my bus just crawled along in traffic, so when a woman asked to get off two blocks later, near Poydras Street, I asked for a transfer and got off too. But a block later something strange happened with that bus stuck in traffic: a policeman told the driver the president had been shot and said no one was to leave the bus until officers talked to the passengers. Then two policemen boarded the bus and checked each passenger for weapons.

Why? Was every bus in a four-block radius around Dealey Plaza stopped and checked for weapons? And the bus was going *toward* Dealey Plaza, not away from it, fifteen minutes after the shooting. Why would an assassin take a bus? Back past the scene of the crime? Carrying a handgun? What kind of sense does that make? But the plotters knew I'd take this bus because they'd told me to go home. If the cops had found me on board the bus, they could have killed me, dropping a "throw-down" handgun, claiming self-defense. Think about it – I'd already been set up as the patsy – this was the second opportunity to eliminate me and close the case. There would be three more setups to kill me in the next hour.

I decided I'd better get a taxi, so I went back to Lamar, turned right and walked to the Greyhound Bus Depot, at the northwest corner of Jackson and Lamar – four blocks. Now, consider: *I was at the Greyhound Bus Depot.* Why didn't I just catch a bus out of town, if I was the assassin? Why would I go back to my room? If I was this vicious killer, why did I leave almost all of my cash for Marina? Where was I going with less than $14 in my pocket?

I got in a taxicab at about 12:48. Driver William Wayne Whaley testified to the WC on March 12, 1964: "He was walking south on Lamar from Commerce...on the west side of the street.... He opened the front door... and got in. He was dressed in just ordinary work clothes.... [His pants] were khaki material...faded blue color. Then he had on a brown shirt with a little silverlike stripe on it... His shirt was open three buttons down here. He had on a T-shirt."

There were two odd things in this Whaley transcript. First, when Whaley was shown a couple of jackets, he *supposedly* said I was wearing two jackets, one on top of the other, which I wasn't, but he'd said nothing about *any*

Neches and Neely.

jacket in his November 23, 1963 affidavit. Second, the transcript repeatedly had him testifying that he'd dropped me off in the 500 block of North Beckley *(just as he'd also sworn in his November 23 affidavit)* – but at the corner of *Neches* Street.

To begin with, Neches didn't go to Beckley, so there was no corner of Beckley and Neches. Then, that area was the 1000 block, not the 500 block. Whaley had driven a taxi in Dallas for 37 years, so he wouldn't make such a mistake. He bragged to the WC, "You name an intersection in the city of Dallas, and I will tell you what is on all four corners." And experienced court reporters don't repeatedly make errors like that. This transcript was altered by the WC.

1. Dobbs House Restaurant,1221 N. Beckley, 2. 1026 N. Beckley (& Zangs), 3. N. Beckley & Neely.

When Whaley testified *again* [Why?!], on April 8, things began to clear up. This time the transcript showed that Whaley said he'd dropped me at the corner of Beckley and *Neely*. The WC attorney asked if that was the 500 block of Beckley – Whaley said it was the 700 block. Then the WC attorney stated that he himself had "…walked back from the point where the Deponent Whaley told us he let the passenger off...[and] this walk took 5 minutes and 45 seconds." *But if Whaley had dropped me at the 500 block, it would have taken me close to ten minutes to arrive at 1026, getting there at 1:04!*

Now things got clear! If Neches *had* butted into Beckley, it would have been almost right across the street from my rooming house! The WC had been trying to cut over six minutes off my travel time – they wanted to place me at my rooming house by 12:54 – trying to get me to Tippit's shooting on time! So, the WC just changed "Neely" to "Neches," failing to substitute the "1000" block for the "500" block in the transcript.

The WC got away with such tricks because often witnesses were not willing to take the time to come back to read and sign the transcripts of their testimonies, so a number of transcripts were altered by the WC, without the witnesses knowing it – one witness claimed his signature had been forged.

So, Whaley, driving south, took me past my rooming house. The first time Whaley testified, he said a re-creation of the trip took nine minutes, meaning I would have arrived there at 12:57 and got to my rooming house at almost 1:03!

The second time he testified, it became five and a half minutes, so we'd have arrived at about 12:54, *if* he'd dropped me off at Neely, not the 500 block of Beckley. But Whaley's manifest showed that he'd dropped me at "500 No. Beckley," so don't bet that I didn't get off at the 500 block, arriving at 1026 at 1:04!

CE 382 (PDF) – Whaley's manifest

I crossed to the east side of the street and walked back toward 1026, checking to see if anyone was following me or if anyone was waiting for me around my rooming house. Don't forget, the CIA had trained me in espionage techniques five years earlier. Why else would I have driven several blocks past 1026?

1026 North Beckley Avenue, in later years.

I hurried into 1026. The housekeeper, Earlene Roberts, stated in an affidavit on December 5, 1963: "At approximately 1:00 P.M. I was sitting in the living room...when...Lee Harvey Oswald came in the front door.... *Oswald did not have a jacket*...and I don't recall what type of clothing he was wearing.

"Oswald went to his room and was only there a very few minutes before coming out. I noticed he had a jacket he was putting on. I recall the jacket was a dark color, and it was the type that zips up the front. He was zipping the jacket up as he left.

"Oswald went out the front door. A moment later I looked out the window. I saw Lee Oswald standing on the curb at the bus stop just to the right and on the same side of the street as our house [*east side*]. Just glanced out the window that once. I don't know how long Lee Oswald

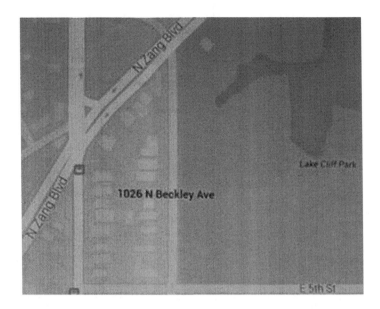

stood at the curb, nor did I see which direction he went when he left there."

Only thirty minutes later, Earlene attested in the affidavit, three Dallas policemen came by, and Earlene let them into my room. This address wasn't on file with the TSBD – how did the cops get it? As they were searching my room, two FBI agents arrived. The police and agents took away everything in the room that belonged to me, Earlene stated. She said nothing about a holster supposedly found in my room and shown to her. But why were my *clothes* taken – and why weren't they itemized, like my shoes were?

On November 29, Earlene had a chat with two FBI

agents, and when she came before the WC on April 8, 1964 some things had become blurred or changed since her affidavit. Asked when I'd come in, Earlene said, "Now, it must have been around 1 o'clock, *or maybe a little after ....what time I wouldn't want to say because –* " [The WC lawyer quickly interrupted her.] "He come in, and I just looked up and I said, 'Oh, you are in a hurry....' He didn't say nothing – he wouldn't say nothing – period.... He went on to his room and stayed about 3 or 4 minutes.... He got a jacket and put it on – it was kind of a zipper jacket."

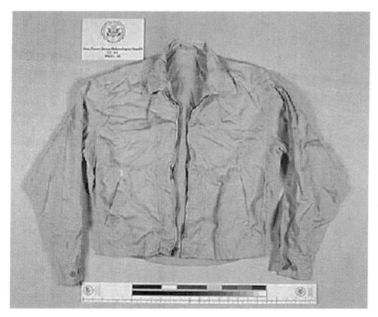

WC Exhibit 162, which looks just like the light brown jacket Officer Baker described on Lee Oswald. However, police and the WC Always called this jacket "gray."

When shown a jacket (above) and asked if she'd ever seen it before, Earlene replied, "Well, maybe I have, but I don't remember it. It seems like the one he put on was *darker than that*. Now, I won't be sure, because *I really don't know*." Of course she didn't – I wasn't wearing a jacket.

Fact is, the WC needed Earlene to put me in that light-colored zipper jacket, which would tie me to the murder of Dallas Police Office J. D. Tippit that was due to happen in a couple of minutes. *No one else ever saw me in any jacket that day.*

In addition, the WC reported, "When he left home [Irving] that morning, Marina Oswald, who was still in bed, [*supposedly*] suggested that he wear a jacket. A blue jacket, later identified by Marina Oswald as her husband's, was subsequently found [*days later*] in the [TSBD] building, apparently left behind by Oswald." No way of telling when it was put there or who put it there, or – considering Marina's track record for telling tall tales – whether I actually owned such a jacket. In any case, this *supposed* jacket didn't matter.

The zipper jacket that Mrs. Roberts *first* 'recalled' was *seemingly* 'my' blue jacket, which the FBI or police must've mentioned to her. Question: how come she didn't remember *anything* about my clothes when I came in but remembered the "kind of a zipper jacket" when I went out? And didn't recall anything else I had on when I left?

Then the WC attorney showed her a picture of *my rust-brown shirt*: [Attorney: 'Have you seen that before?'] "Well, maybe I have. Now, that looks kind of like the dark shirt that he had on." [Attorney: 'When Oswald came in, he was in a shirt – does this shirt look anything like the shirt he had on?'] "It was a dark shirt he had on – I think it was a dark one...." So, she didn't remember what clothes I had on coming in but did remember the shirt and jacket – *after* the WC attorney nudged her.

Earlene later made two comments: "I want you to understand that I have been put through the third degree, and it's hard to remember," also said, "Well, you know, I can't see too good how to read. I'm completely blind in my right eye." For an older lady, it certainly was hard to remember information that the FBI agents fed her.

Then, ['You were working there...last fall – 1963?'] "Yes, to my sorrows." ['Why to your sorrows?'] "Well, he was registered as O. H. Lee, and I come to find out he was Oswald – and I wish I had never known it." ['Why?']

"Well, they put me through the third degree." ['Who did?'] "The FBI, Secret Service, [Captain] Will Fritz's men and [Sheriff] Bill Decker's." But, wait, that's not all! "I had worked for some policemen and sometimes they come by and tell me something that maybe their wives would want me to know...." So, she was friendly with two Dallas cops, too – and what are friends for except to be friendly? Much of her testimony is suspect.

Earlene also testified that just after I'd come in, she heard two beeps of a car's horn, and when she "just glanced out" her *front window*, she saw a black police car – which she initially said was #207 – with two uniformed men in it. "And then...they just went on around the corner [of Zangs]." Further in her testimony she said, "[The car] stopped directly in front of my house...and *I went to the door* and looked...." The Dallas Police Department was never able to identify who the two men and the car were.

The WC lawyer told Earlene that "[Oswald] **_might_** have had a pistol or a revolver," to which Earlene replied that she hadn't seen and had never known about a gun in my room. However, after the police searched my room, she testified, they *supposedly* came out with a holster, which she'd never seen before. Funny, how things kept turning up later to try to incriminate me. Now, where did I buy that *imaginary* holster, and did the police/FBI really show her a holster?

Earlene also told the WC, "He stayed home every night – I didn't ever know of him going out.... He was always home at night – he never went out." So, then I guess the 'Oswald' who was in Jack Ruby's Carousel Club some nights wasn't me, but Lee. And stop to consider: if I was in my room every night and went to Irving every Friday and came back every Monday morning, and ate lunch in the TSBD every day, how much possible conspiring could I have been doing?

The WC noted that I'd changed clothes in my room, because they were dirty. Earlene said I was there no more than 3 to 4 minutes. Let's see how that might have gone down. I walk in the front door, pass Earlene in the living room, go to my room, unlock the door, open the door, close the door, sit on my bed, unlace my right shoe and take it off, unlace my left shoe and take it off, remove my belt, remove from my pants pockets and put on my bed my wallet, eighty-seven cents in change, thirteen dollars in paper money, and a key for a P.O. Box.

When I was arrested, police also found in my pants

pockets a small white box top with the name "Cox's, Fort Worth" and a paycheck stub from American Bakeries (which, it was later found, had once been attached to a check made out to one James Jackson, a real person), dated August 22, 1960 – when I was in Russia. Now, where would I have gotten these two items and why would I have had them in my pants pockets? If they'd been in my pockets when I entered my room, that would mean I'd taken them out to Irving the previous afternoon. If I hadn't taken them out to Irving, I'd have had to pick them up from my room now. What for? Both look like trash – odd trash, but trash. I'll talk about them later.

To continue: I stand up, unbutton and unzip and drop my pants ("faded blue color"), sit down and pull off the right leg of my pants, pull off the left leg, go get another pair of pants (dark), take it off its hanger, sit on the bed, pull on one leg and then the other, stand up and button and zip my pants, put on my belt, put my wallet and all coins and paper money and P.O. box key into my pants pockets, get a pair of loafers and slip them on. But I don't take off my brown shirt. Why? Wasn't *it* dirty? And I deliberately leave the shirt hanging out.

I get my *supposed* zip jacket and put it on over my

brown shirt (which I was arrested in and which still had in its pocket the bus transfer given to me by bus driver Cecil J. McWatters), go to a dresser, pull open a drawer – I don't take out a pistol because I don't have one, don't have bullets, either – and reach into the drawer to get the box top and check stub and put them in a pants pocket. If I had on a jacket, why wouldn't I have put those in a jacket pocket?

I go to the door, open it, step out, close it, lock it, start walking out, pass Earlene while *supposedly* zipping up the jacket, open the front door, go out, close the door, walk across the porch, down two steps, down the cement path (25'-30' long) to the sidewalk, turn right, go (10'-15') to a bus stop and stand there – all in just over three minutes, believe it or not! Not.

But, wait! I was arrested wearing my brown shirt, so my dark brown shirt tails – hanging outside my pants below my jacket – should have been obvious to Earlene. But…she said she didn't notice anything but my jacket. Note that *no one* up to now except Marion Baker claims I was wearing a light brown windbreaker.

One more thing: Earlene said I went out and stood at a bus stop, which was *north* of 1026. Why? I obviously didn't plan to take a bus back to Dealey Plaza – I wound up in the Texas Theatre three or four minutes later. And if I'd walked to East 10th Street and Patton (why, if I was a "lone nut"?!), like the WC claimed, I'd have gone down the path from 1026, turned *left* and walked *south*, and Earlene never would have seen me when she glanced out her window. I must have been waiting for someone to pick me up - *but it wasn't Police Officer J. D. Tippit!*

Shooting of J. D. Tippit

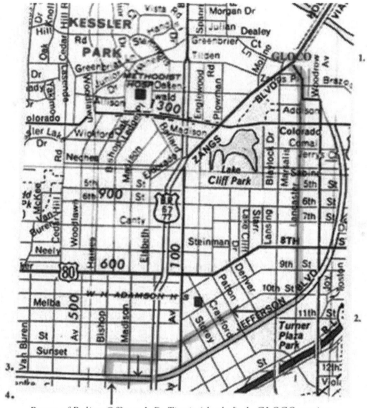

Route of Police Officer J. D. Tippit (shaded). 1. GLOCO station, 2. Tippit shooting, 3. Texas Theatre, 4. Top Ten Record Store

A few minutes before I got to my rooming house, as Whaley was driving me southwest on Zangs Boulevard, his taxi passed by Tippit at the Gloco gas station. Tippit was seen by five witnesses in his patrol car watching westbound traffic for ten minutes, from about 12:45 on. He must've been waiting for the "Marsalis" bus that I'd been on, but when the bus didn't show, Tippit left the gas station and drove rapidly south on Lancaster, ironically the same street and direction that Lee had driven a few minutes earlier.

Top Ten Record Shop, Bishop Street at right.

At 12:54 P.M., Tippit radioed his position as "Lancaster and 8th Street." He continued on and turned right on Jefferson, then drove to the Top Ten Record Store, 338 West Jefferson, a block and a half west of the Texas Theatre, on the south side of Jefferson, near Bishop Street.

He parked his car on Bishop, hurriedly entered the store and asked to use the store's phone. Tippit said nothing while his number kept ringing, finally hung up the phone, looking worried or upset. Why the phone call? It sure wasn't police business – Tippit's radio was working fine. What did he want to ask, or report? And to who? And why hadn't he tried phoning from the Gloco station?

Tippit hurried out to his patrol car and drove across Jefferson, then one block north on Bishop, turned right on Sunset and left on Zangs. When he saw a car heading west on 10th Street cross Zangs, he turned left on 10th behind it. James A. Andrews later said he was driving west on West 10th Street, just after 1:00 P.M., when – about two blocks northwest of the Top Ten Record Shop – a police car suddenly passed him and cut in front of his car at an angle and stopped, forcing him to brake.

The police officer jumped out of his car, motioned for Andrews to stay put, then ran back to Andrews' car and looked in the space between the front and back seats. Perplexed, Andrews noted the officer's nameplate, which read "Tippit." Tippit seemed very upset and agitated, Andrews said, and was "acting wild." Without saying a word, Tippit returned to his car and drove off rapidly.

Tippit must have made a U-turn, then crossed Beckley – right after the time I entered my rooming house. But why was Tippit concerned about 10th Street? What did he hope or expect to find on 10th? Of all the streets in Oak Cliff, *why this one? He had to have a reason, a need. Who was he looking for – on that street?* He hadn't been radioed to search for any suspect. *Who* was he after, if not *me*?

The WC asked three senior Dallas police officers if they could explain Tippit's movements. Not only could none of them offer a reasonable explanation, but none of them was even aware that the dispatcher *supposedly* ordered Tippit to the Oak Cliff neighborhood. Tippit wasn't ordered there, so what was he doing there?

Me, Lee and Tippit, at about 1:02 P.M.

A time check: I *supposedly* stayed in my rooming house for three to four minutes, went outside and stood at the curb by the bus stop, which had to have taken at least 1 minute, since Earlene didn't see me moving. That places me in front of my rooming house between 1:04 and 1:05 at the earliest, maybe four minutes later, if Whaley dropped me off at 500 N. Beckley.

To put this into perspective: Dallas County Deputy Sheriff Roger Craig later wrote:

"An unknown Dallas police officer came running up the stairs [at the TSBD] and advised Capt. [Will] Fritz that a Dallas policeman had been shot in the Oak Cliff area. I instinctively looked at my watch. The time was 1:06 P.M....

"The Dallas [police] dispatcher called Tippit at 1:04 P.M. and received no answer. He continued to call three times and there was still no reply. Comparing this time with the time I received news of the shooting of the police officer at 1:06 P.M., it is fair to assume Tippit was dead or being killed between 1:04 and 1:06 P.M. This is also corroborated by the eyewitnesses at the Tippit killing, who said he was shot between 1:05 and 1:08 P.M."

Dallas Police Officer Bob L. Carroll seems to corroborate Craig: "[About what time did you get to the School Book Depository?] "I believe it was approximately 1 o'clock – maybe a little before, but right around 1 o'clock, and after I got [there]...I was assigned to search the basement but... I went into the basement and we determined that we needed some light...and when I got [back] upstairs I heard that an officer had been shot in Oak Cliff." That sure seems like a 1:06-1:08 time frame.

The scene of the Tippit shooting was *over nine blocks away* (.9 of a mile) from my rooming house (see map on p. 190), so I couldn't have been there. Of course, the WC claimed Tippit was shot at 1:16, which he wasn't. But we'll get to that soon.

Now, how long did it take to drive Lee to Oak Cliff in the Rambler, leaving at 12:40 P.M. from Dealey Plaza? It *supposedly* was a six (or nine) minute drive to my rooming house, but November 22 was a Friday afternoon, and traffic was heavier that day, so Lee got to where he was going at about 12:50. However, Lee didn't go to the "safe house" on North Beckley, in any case, because he was spotted, by 1:00 P.M., less than three blocks northwest from Jack Ruby's apartment, walking west on East 10th Street, three blocks east of where Tippit would be shot. Where was Lee coming from? And why wasn't he in hiding or getting out of town, like all the other assassins?

The previous night, a guest of Jack Ruby's next door

1. Tippit shooting, 410 East 10th, 2. Jack Ruby's apartment, 223 S. Ewing, 3. Texas Theatre, 231 West Jefferson.

neighbor who had answered her friend's door encountered Lee asking for Ruby. Why was Lee dropped off in that general area the next afternoon, rather than near the Texas Theatre? Was there another "safe house," on East 10th Street? Did Lee pick up a jacket and make a quick phone call? Did he change his pants? Why else would he be in that neighborhood? He had at least ten minutes.

Soon after 1:00 P.M., a barber at 620 East 10th Street, the south side of the street, saw Lee pass by his shop, heading west *in a great hurry*. The barber believed it was "Lee Harvey Oswald." I was at my rooming house at that time. Lee walked past the Town and Country Cafe at 604 East 10th, crossed Marsalis Avenue (one block west of Lancaster), and continued west. A minute or two later, William Lawrence Smith, walking east toward the Town and Country Cafe for lunch, said he was sure the man who walked by him was "Lee Harvey Oswald." I was still at my rooming house at that time.

Another witness, William Arthur Smith, who said he saw Lee walking west, described him as "a white male…150-160 lbs….dark hair…wearing a white shirt, *light brown jacket and dark pants.*" Where was Lee going? He wasn't coming from Ruby's apartment – Ruby wasn't there, and if Lee had been headed straight to the Texas Theatre, he most likely would have walked west on Jefferson Avenue than west on East 10th Street.

As Lee got near Patton, Tippit, driving east on East 10th, slowly pulled over to near the curb by Lee, who casually walked over to the patrol car and began speaking with Tippit through the passenger side vent window. This was in front of 410 East 10th. Although Lee put his hands on the patrol car, *supposedly* no fingerprints were recovered. One witness said it seemed like Tippit and Lee knew each other. Keep in mind that Lee and Tippit had been seen at the same time at the Dobbs House Restaurant two mornings earlier.

No one will ever know what really took place, so everyone will have to come to their own conclusion. Here's my take on what happened: when Lee began talking with Tippit, he realized Tippit thought Lee was me, and when Tippit started getting out of the car Lee assumed Tippit would kill him, mistaking Lee for me. Lee drew his gun first and fired across the hood of the car, striking Tippit three times in the chest. Lee started to leave, still going west, but then went around the car to Tippit. He had to make sure Tippit was dead, so Lee put a fourth bullet in Tippit's head. As Lee hurried away, one witness heard him mutter, "Poor dumb cop." A second Shakespearean tragedy in Dallas in thirty-five minutes.

Let's try to figure out what was *supposed* to happen – if I wasn't killed in the TSBD – and what went wrong. I was told to take a bus home after I left the TSBD and meet my handler at the Texas Theatre by 1:20. I believe Tippit was supposed to apprehend and kill me when I got off the bus.

But when traffic got heavy, I left the bus, which prevented my being shot on the bus, the second opportunity to kill me. When the bus remained stuck in traffic and didn't arrive in Oak Cliff, that prevented the third opportunity to kill me – if I'd gotten off the bus there. When Tippit finally saw 'Lee Harvey Oswald,' he wasn't careful enough and got killed. If I wasn't slated to be killed there, why was Tippit in that neighborhood and why did he stop Lee? There just isn't any other logical reason. It's ridiculous to believe he stopped Lee thinking he was a suspect in JFK's murder. The description broadcast was too vague, and what would the killer be doing there?

Now, I don't want to talk about the weapon used and the shells found at the Tippit murder scene, because I wasn't there. But there are things I *do* want to look at: the time of the murder, the descriptions of the killer, and 'my' wallet and its contents at the scene.

I've already shown you that *I didn't have the time to walk to Patton and 10th from my rooming house to kill Tippit*. There also was a witness, Mrs. Donald Higgins, at 417 East 10th Street, who was *not* called by the WC – for obvious reasons. She heard three or four shots that day, then some screaming, ran to her front door, saw a policeman lying in the street and a man with a gun running toward Patton Street.

Asked in March of 1968 by assassination researcher Barry Ernest when all this began happening, Mrs. Higgins said a moment after 1:06. How was she so sure? She was watching television, she said, and the newscaster turned to look at his clock and said it was six minutes after one, right

Shooting of J. D. Tippit

before the shots. That sure was not what the WC wanted to hear, so Mrs. Higgins wasn't asked to testify.

Witness T. F. Bowley, who arrived *after* the shooting, stated that he "...saw a police officer lying next to the left front wheel. I looked at my watch, and it said 1:10 P.M. Several people were at the scene.... The police arrived and...I told him I did not witness the shooting." *Several people already at the scene would put the shooting around 1:06-1:08.*

Witness Helen Markham, heading to work, left her home at 328 East Ninth Street "a little after 1:00," going to catch her regular 1:15 work bus at Patton and Jefferson. She had walked about one block south on Patton, to the northwest corner of Patton and East 10th, when she saw the shooting. Asked about the time, she said, "I wouldn't be afraid to bet it wasn't 6 or 7 minutes after 1:00."

Next, a description of the killer and his clothes by some of the witnesses:

William W. Scoggins: [...what kind of trousers...?] "They was dark, not too dark, and he had on a light shirt.... a pistol in his *left hand*."

Helen Markham: "He had these dark trousers on....a

short jacket open in the front, kind of a grayish tan."

Virginia Davis: [...color his trousers?] " I think they were black. Brown jacket...."

Barbara J. Davis: [...a shirt...Commission Exhibit No. 150] "The shirt he had on was lighter than that." [Color of his hair?] "Either dark brown or black. It was just dark hair." [...color of his clothes?] "He...had on dark trousers, and a light colored shirt, with a dark coat over it."

Ted Callaway: "...dark trousers and a light tannish gray windbreaker jacket..., fair complexion, dark hair..., about 5'10"." [...a jacket here, Commission's Exhibit No. 162.] "That is the same type jacket...it had a little more tan to it.... He looked to me like around 160 pounds.... Just a nice athletic type...."

Domingo Benavides: The killer was 5'10"-5'11", and "I remember the back of his head...looked like his hairline sort of went square instead of tapered off. And he looked like he needed a haircut for about two weeks, but his hair didn't taper off, it kind of went down and *squared off* and made his head look flat in back." Remember who got haircuts like that? Lee, of course.

Also recall officer Marrion L. Baker's description: *"A white man, approximately 30 years old, 5'9", 165 pounds, dark hair, wearing a light brown jacket."*

However, it was Mrs. Higgins who put the last nail in the coffin to bury the notion that *I'd* shot Tippit, for when Barry Ernest asked her if that man was Lee Harvey Oswald, she answered with a sigh, "He definitely was not the man they showed on television."

When Lee got near Patton, he cut across the grass of the corner house, continued on the east side of Patton, then ran across to the west side, still with the gun in his hand. He turned right on East Jefferson Avenue, slipped the gun into his pants at his waist and slowed to a walk.

As he got to Ballew's Texaco Service Station, one block west, at Jefferson and Crawford Streets, on the northeast corner of Jefferson, he ran – north – behind the station and was last seen in the parking lot directly in back of the station, probably continuing west in the alley behind the parking lot.

A windbreaker jacket, *supposedly* belonging to the killer – described variously as light grey or white or light brown, was *supposedly* found under a car in the Ballew parking lot by an *unidentified* policeman a little later. The jacket was a "medium" size – I wore "small" – and the jacket's laundry and dry cleaning tags couldn't be traced to any laundry or cleaning establishment in the Dallas or New Orleans areas – because if it *was* Lee's or the Rambler driver's, they both had lived in Florida. And Marina had never sent my jackets to a dry cleaner – she washed them.

Police Captain W. R. Westbrook holding the wallet.

Now we come to 'my' wallet, which appeared and disappeared mysteriously at the Tippit murder scene. *Supposedly*, the killer handed his *entire* wallet to Tippit through the *rolled down* passenger window – despite the fact that witness Virginia Davis said the passenger window was *rolled up*, despite the Dallas police homicide report (next page), despite the police photographs of the patrol car, showing the window *rolled up*.

But who hands their entire wallet to a police officer, anyway? And why? Plus a police officer wouldn't make

"...they talked through the closed window...."

such a request – he wouldn't want to be responsible for the contents of someone's wallet. And a killer so thoughtless that he forgets about the wallet he handed to a policeman moments before he shot him to death?

At around 1:15 P.M. an ambulance was dispatched from the Dudley Hughes Funeral Home and arrived at 10th and Patton within a minute. Dallas Police Reserve Sergeant Kenneth H. Croy testified he arrived at the Tippit murder scene as the ambulance was picking up Tippit's body. So,

Croy arrived at the earliest at 1:17. Croy told an interviewer that *an unknown man handed him 'Oswald's' wallet right after his arrival*. Why didn't Croy immediately radio in the names on the IDs in the wallet? This was the murder of a policeman, after all, with the killer running loose.

Ted Callaway and other citizen witnesses responded to the scene. None of them saw a wallet on the ground. Callaway said, "There was no billfold on the scene. If there was, there would have been too many people who would have seen it." The wallet could only have been *brought to the scene* by someone.

The wallet was photographed by a TV cameraman, *at 1:42 P.M.* What did Sergeant Croy do with the wallet – *supposedly* handed him by "an unknown man" – between 1:17 and 1:42, twenty-five minutes? And where did that wallet go after 1:42? No one would say. Nor did the WC ask Sgt. Croy about the wallet. Why? A police detective was supposedly talking with an FBI agent about the wallet at the time it was photographed. For years, that FBI agent gave a tortured cock and bull story about the wallet.

The wallet was a "throw-down" to frame me, just as police have used throw-down guns to frame people. It was to provide quick identification of me, so I'd be tied to the

Tippit murder immediately. The wallet was there in case I wasn't caught at the Texas Theatre a half hour later. When I was arrested at the theater, with a wallet, the Tippit scene wallet 'vanished.' That wallet *supposedly* contained two IDs, one *supposedly* for Lee Harvey Oswald, the other *supposedly* for Alek J. Hidell. No Dallas cop ever wrote a report about this magical appearing and disappearing wallet.

Doppelgänger: The Legend Of Lee Harvey Oswald

The Rifle(s)

Meanwhile, at 1:00 P.M., Dallas police officers were filmed removing a rifle from the roof of the TSBD. The rifle had no sling, no scope, and the barrel protruded at least 7-8 inches past the stock. In the film, two police officers were seen standing on a fire escape at the seventh floor of the Depository, gesturing toward the roof. Then the film showed the rifle being examined.

A few minutes after 1:00, *Fort Worth Star-Telegram* reporter Thayer Waldo watched a group of high-ranking Dallas police officers huddle together for a conference at the TSBD. When he later spoke with a police secretary who knew about the officers' conversations, she told him they'd found a rifle "on the roof of the School Book Depository." The rifle was never seen again, never mentioned. But consider how it may have gotten on the roof. It probably was there the whole time, if Baker and Truly never went up to the roof!

At 1:22 P.M., Deputy Constable Seymour Weitzman

found a 7.65 German Mauser bolt action rifle, with a 4/18 scope and a thick leather sling (the 'sling' of 'my' rifle originally belonged to a pistol shoulder holster), in the northwest corner of the TSBD's sixth floor, between some boxes *near the stairway* – just where Lee's spotter had left it. Weitzman and Deputy Sheriff E. L. Boone, both men with above average knowledge of weapons, as well as Deputy Sheriff Roger Craig and Capt. Will Fritz, identified the make of the rifle, Craig stating that he saw "765 Mauser" stamped into the metal of the rifle. Then, at 1:37 P.M. Fort Worth's WBAP reported: "Crime Lieutenant J. C. Day just came out of that building. Reported British .303 rifle with telescopic lens." A photo of him holding the rifle was published the next day.

By late afternoon, however, the weapon mysteriously had turned into a 6.5 mm Italian Carcano, which was *supposedly* found on the sixth floor. However, ATF agent Frank Ellsworth claimed the Carcano "was not found on

A 7.65 Mauser at top, a 6.5 mm Carcano below it.

The Rifle(s)

Supposedly 'my' rifle, in the National Archives.

Photo of 'my' rifle taken by Dallas police.

the same floor as the cartridges, but on a lower floor, by a couple of city detectives.... I think the rifle was found on the *fourth floor*," which means it was probably planted there ahead of time.

Although *supposedly* sent from Crescent Firearms to Klein's Sporting Goods in Chicago, that particular rifle was never shipped to Klein's. My order was never received by Klein's, because I never sent it – I was at work on March 12, 1963 when the 'order' was 'mailed.' Klein's had no record of the order. The 'order coupon' furnished to the WC was forged, showing that "A. J. Hidell" had sent it. Obviously, it didn't have my fingerprints on it. 'My' rifle was 40" long, but the ad and coupon were for a 36" Carcano – Klein's didn't even sell a 40" Carcano rifle at that time.

'My' postal money order was never deposited in a bank by Klein's. My Dallas P.O. box application never listed "Hidell," and the post office wasn't allowed to deliver a weapon to anyone not listed on the form. I couldn't have been given a rifle by the P.O. *without filling out postal form 2162, required to be filled out by <u>both</u> the shipper and the receiver of a firearm.* No such forms were ever found. No Dallas postal worker ever saw the imaginary long package with a rifle in it. By the way, a postal inspector involved in my case was an FBI informant. He even sat in on one of my interrogations. Does that tell you something?

I didn't order a rifle, I didn't receive a rifle, I didn't take a rifle to New Orleans, I didn't bring back a rifle from New Orleans – I first went to Mexico City before coming back to Dallas. There was no rifle in Ruth Paine's garage – neither she nor her husband Michael ever saw a rifle. Marina lied to the WC when she said I had a rifle – *no one else ever claimed to have seen 'my' rifle.* No one ever saw me with a four-foot-long package, or any package, in the TSBD. My fingerprints were not on the rifle, although a

The Rifle(s)

palm print taken from my dead body was 'found' *days later, supposedly* on a hidden surface of the barrel. Never any proof of that – the fingerprint technician told a very fishy story. No fingerprints on the "bag" in which 'my' rifle was *supposedly* placed. No indications 'my' rifle ever was in the "bag" – no gun oil nor indentations on the paper.

In WC testimony, experts called the rifle "a very cheap rifle," "real cheap, common, real flimsy-looking," "a piece of junk," "…very easily knocked out of adjustment." This imported Carcano came from a lot of defective rifles which could be bought for $3.00 apiece in lots of 25. It was a manual bolt-action rifle, which could not fire two rounds in 1.7 seconds. It wasn't possible to accurately fire three rounds in 5.6 seconds, even by the most expert riflemen. The rifle had a worn and rusty firing pin. No ammunition clip for the rifle was found on November 22, and without it a shooter would have had to hand-feed the ammunition, which couldn't be done in 5.6 seconds and would make aiming very difficult.

The rifle couldn't be sighted by experts because the scope was too wobbly – it had to be repaired before the gun could be test fired. The FBI wrote to the WC that the telescopic sight could not be properly aligned with the target, since the sight reached the limit of its adjustment before reaching accurate alignment. Ammunition for a Carcano would often hang fire – it was last made at the end of World War II. JFK was killed by high velocity rifles – the Carcano was not high velocity.

I could go on about the Carcano, but I think this is enough, especially since *it wasn't my rifle*. Bottom line, *no one fired that rifle on November 22, 1963*. It was planted, before or after the shooting. Years later, Dallas police chief Jesse Curry told newsmen, "We don't have any proof that Oswald fired the rifle, and never did. Nobody's yet been able to put him in that building with a gun in his hand."

Texas Theatre – Lies & Liars

The Texas Theatre, 1963

The Texas Theatre is at 231 West Jefferson Boulevard, 1.05 miles from 1026 North Beckley, driving time 2-3 minutes (down Zangs), walking time (by a young adult male) 18 minutes. So, I couldn't have walked to the Texas Theatre that afternoon – someone must've driven me, getting me there at 1:07-1:08. Who drove me? The two "policemen" in the black "police" car? Or? Whichever car it was, I was in it when Tippit was being shot. But why was it so important for me to get to the Texas Theatre – right at that time – that I had to be driven?

Also need another time check – how long it would've taken the killer of Officer Tippit to walk from the murder scene to the Texas Theatre. That distance is about .7 of a mile, including the detour to the back of the Texaco gas station and the later return to Jefferson Boulevard. Normal walking time over that distance for a young man would be about 13 minutes. Allowing for Lee's earlier jogging away from the crime scene, let's lower that to 11 minutes. Lee likely began leaving the crime scene at about 1:08, so adding 11 minutes brings the time of arrival at the theater to 1:19 at the earliest, *if* Lee didn't stop on the way – which he may have. Now, *if* Officer Tippit *had* been killed at 1:16, as the WC falsely claimed, then Tippit's killer would have reached the theater around 1:27 P.M., at the earliest, which time is twenty minutes after I got there.

The WC said I sneaked into the theatre – not true. *I bought a ticket!* What possible reason would I have for sneaking in – I had money in my pocket. Why would I draw attention to myself by sneaking into a theater at midday like a ten-year-old? Please remember I was trained in spycraft by the CIA. I wouldn't do something that dumb.

The theater's cashier, Julia Postal, was interviewed by researcher Jones Harris in '63. When asked if she'd sold a ticket to "Oswald," Julia burst into tears and left the room. Asked again a little later if she'd sold a ticket to "Oswald," she burst into tears once more. Her reactions and refusal to answer this question indicate that she *did* sell me a ticket. *I didn't sneak into the theater!*

Twenty-two-year-old Warren "Butch" Burroughs, who took tickets and ran the theater's concession stand, *was never asked* by the WC for *any time estimates*. The only 'relevant' things he *supposedly* said to the WC were, "[Did you see that man come in the theatre?] "No, sir; I didn't.... I *think* he sneaked up the stairs real fast." [Up to the balcony?] "Yes, sir – first, I *think* he was up there." [When the police came.... What did you tell him?] "I said, 'I *haven't seen him* myself. He *might have*, but *I didn't see him* when he came in. *He must have sneaked in and run on upstairs before I saw him.*'" "I think...I think...might have...must have..." – those are not *facts*. Butch wasn't asked and said nothing about selling me popcorn – and he later contradicted what he *supposedly* told the WC, which barely questioned Butch. I'll show you why soon.

Butch later told assassination researchers that he knew

that "Oswald" had come in "between 1:00 and 1:07," because he had seen him soon after that. Butch also volunteered that he had sold him popcorn at 1:15. Now, would a crazed amateur killer, who in the last forty-five minutes had murdered in cold blood the President of the United States and a Dallas police officer and had snuck into a theatre to hide, *come back down* from the balcony a few minutes later to buy popcorn? Then go and sit in the orchestra? And Butch doesn't realize he didn't take a ticket from this man, although there are only about a dozen people in the orchestra, in a theater seating 900? Does that make any kind of sense?

By now it should be obvious that witnesses were pressured to say what the FBI or WC wanted said, that transcripts of testimonies were tampered with, and that evidence was manufactured and altered. There's also testimony which is so confusing that it's hard to know what to make of it.

In any case, I had to find my contact, so I went into the orchestra. I *sat next* to a young man, later identified as Jack Davis, when the movie presentation began – shortly before 1:20 P.M., he later said – and waited for a prearranged signal.

Now, if you've been wondering why I had a paycheck stub from American Bakeries dated August 22, 1960 – when I was in Russia – and a small white box top with the name "Cox's, Fort Worth" in my pockets, consider whether one or both of these were part of my prearranged signal for my contact. My contact could have had the bottom of the box, perhaps the cancelled check to match the stub. Why else would I be carrying these? They were trash, otherwise. Nothing that I'd keep, or carry around with me.

When Jack Davis gave no signal, I got up and *sat beside* another man across the aisle, waited for the signal, again failed to get it, so I went to the lobby briefly. When I returned, I *sat next to* two more people, the last a pregnant woman, waited for the signal once more, but still didn't get it. Why not? Because I was supposed to be dead by now – killed on the bus or at the bus stop where I'd been expected to get off. And consider why I would repeatedly sit right next to people in an almost empty theater, if I wasn't looking for a contact.

We now get to an event whose time line the WC didn't ask for and the witness didn't volunteer. This witness was twenty-two-year-old Johnny Calvin Brewer, manager of Hardy's Shoe Store, 213 West Jefferson, *nine street*

Aerial view, 231 West Jefferson Avenue (far left), about 220 feet distant from 213, east wall to east wall.

numbers east of the Texas Theatre. His WC testimony somehow doesn't seem quite right – "funny," like the man Johnny said he saw in front of his store.

He told the WC on April 2, 1964, that he'd been listening to a transistor radio about JFK being shot, followed by the news that a police officer had been killed in Oak Cliff. Then he heard a police siren. "I looked up and saw the man enter the lobby [the entryway]…and he stood there with his back to the street….[About how far were you from the front door?] "Ten feet…. I heard the police cars coming up Jefferson, and he stepped in, and the police made a U-turn…at Zangs…and went back down East Jefferson. And when they…left, [the man] looked over his shoulder and turned around and walked up West Jefferson…." How could Johnny tell they made a U-turn at Zangs? He was inside the store, at least fifteen feet from the sidewalk, about a hundred feet from the corner of Zangs.

"He was a little man, about 5'9", and weighed about 150 pounds....brown hair. He had a brown sports shirt on. His shirt tail was out." [Any jacket?] "No." [What color of trousers?] "I don't remember." [Light or dark?] "I don't remember that either." [Any other clothing...?] "He had a T-shirt underneath his shirt." [Was his shirt buttoned up all the way?] "A couple of buttons were unbuttoned at the time." [Why did you happen to watch [him]?] "He just looked funny to me."

This was the first stage of Johnny's 'experience.' There are three problems with this part of his account. First is his immediate belief that he was seeing a dangerous person. Johnny didn't tell the WC he suspected the man had killed Tippit, but in an affidavit, given on *December 2*, 1963, Johnny stated that he noticed the man "because he acted so nervous, and I thought at the time he might be the man that had shot the policeman."

The second problem is the time of this event. In his *December 2* affidavit, Johnny stated, "About 1:30 P.M. I saw a man *standing* in the lobby of the shoe store." Researcher Joseph McBride has written that the *earliest* commercial radio report of Tippit's shooting was at 1:26 P.M. – so exactly *when did Johnny hear* the report of

Tippit's death on his transistor radio? And *what was said*? Four months later, testifying before the WC, there was no mention of the time Johnny saw the "funny" man. In any case, I'd been in the Texas Theatre for more than twenty minutes by 1:30.

Third problem was Johnny's description of my brown shirt and white T-shirt, along with no description of my pants. Why did he say that? Let's not forget that *ten days had gone by before his December 2 affidavit*. The man who Johnny *may* have seen in the entryway could have been Lee, who, of course, wasn't wearing a brown shirt. Was Johnny asked by someone to change his description of the man? I don't know. All I know is that there wasn't anyone wearing my brown shirt in the lobby of Johnny's store at 1:30. That shirt was then on my back in the Texas Theatre. *If* anyone *did* duck into the shoe store lobby at 1:30, and into the Texas Theatre at about 1:34, it was Lee, not me.

And remember that several witnesses at the Tippit murder scene had generally described seeing a white male, dark hair, 160 lbs., 5'10"-5'11", dark trousers, *light-colored shirt*, light grayish/tan windbreaker. *Not one mention of a dark rust-brown long-sleeved tweed shirt with the shirt tail hanging out.* I told you earlier: keep your eyes on my rust-brown shirt.

Let's move on to the second stage of Johnny Brewer's 'experience.' But first: Johnny had arranged to take this day off from work, and his assistant had agreed to take charge. However, the assistant phoned Brewer to say his newborn baby was ill and he couldn't come in. So, Brewer came to work that Friday.

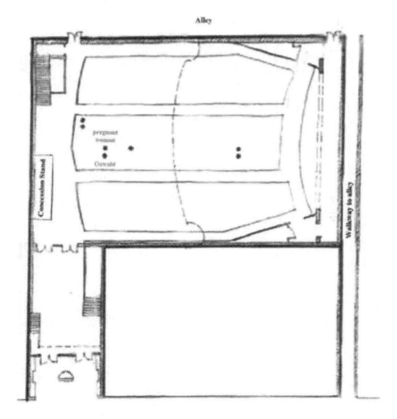

Front entrance of Texas Theatre is at left.

Continuing: Johnny walked out of his store to the sidewalk (at least 15 feet), and *watched the "funny" man walk about 220 feet (73 yards)*, then "[the man] *walked* into the Texas Theatre, and I walked up to the theater – [without hesitation, leaving his store unattended and unlocked?!] – to the box office and asked Mrs. Postal if she sold a ticket to a man who was wearing a brown shirt, and she said no, she hadn't. She was listening to the radio herself. And I said that a man walked in there, and I was going to go inside and ask the usher if he had seen him."

OK, we've deduced that Julia Postal *had* sold me a ticket, so now we can see that someone was orchestrating Julia's and Johnny's testimonies. Many, maybe all, witnesses went through their accounts with an FBI agent or WC attorney prior to testifying before the WC, so there is no way to determine how many accounts came out different in front of the WC – or how many transcripts were changed afterwards.

So, then, the manager of a shoe store, 220 feet east of the Texas Theatre, *supposedly* notices a man in his store's lobby who looks "funny." He comes out of his store to watch this "funny" man *walk* – not trot, not jog, not run, not rush, not dash – *220 feet* west and then *supposedly* "duck" behind the east wall of the theater entrance. Of course, the "funny" man could have been looking at the movie posters on either side of the ticket booth. Why would Johnny immediately assume the man had gone into the theater without paying? And what did Julia Postal mean by "he *ducked* into the theater," especially *since she testified she didn't see the man "duck" in*?

Johnny went on: "So I walked in and Butch Burroughs…was behind the [concession] counter….and I asked him if he had seen a man in a brown shirt…and he said he…hadn't seen anybody." [Not true!] "And I asked him if he would come with me and show me where the exits were, and we would check the exits. And he asked me why. I told him that I thought the guy looked suspicious…. We walked down to the front of the theater to the stage. First we checked the front exit, and it hadn't been opened. We went to the back, and it hadn't been opened." Now, actually, Butch *had* to have seen me, since I bought a ticket and went to sit in the orchestra, not the balcony.

But why even check the exits? Since the concession stand was in the same space as the orchestra seating, if anyone had opened an exit door – it was mid-day – Butch would immediately have seen the light from the alley, and the door could not have shut and locked automatically if opened. Didn't it make more sense to first check if the "funny" man had gone up to the balcony, since Butch couldn't see those stairs from his concession stand?

Going on, "We went back up front and went in the balcony and looked around but we couldn't see anything …we never did see him. But we went back and upstairs and checked, and we came down and went back to the box office and told Julia that we hadn't seen him, and she called the police." If Johnny was so concerned, why didn't he check the men's room too? That's a great place to hide.

After checking upstairs and downstairs, and supposedly *not seeing* the man – in an almost empty theater, you call the police because a store manager nine doors down tells you a man who "looked funny" hadn't paid for a 90¢ theater ticket? Is that what Julia told the police operator when she called? And why would Julia agree to call the police anyway? Based on what? She said she *didn't* see me "duck in." And what would Johnny have *done* if he *had* found the man? Johnny must have believed the man was armed and dangerous. The story doesn't pass the smell test.

Meanwhile *I've been in the orchestra the whole time*, sitting three rows down from the back and five seats left into the center section from the right aisle, and Lee's been up in the balcony. Why wouldn't Johnny have seen me? I was in plain sight – no one even sitting around me by then – the pregnant woman had left. Maybe it was because Johnny had actually seen and was looking for a 'Lee Harvey Oswald' wearing just a white T-shirt, not with a rust-brown tweed shirt over it. So, why didn't he see Lee in the balcony then? He makes no mention of who he saw up there.

Let's hear the third segment of Johnny's 'experience': "Butch went to the front exit [of the orchestra], and I went down by the stage to the back exit and stood there...." Wait a second, didn't it seem that the "funny" man had gone up to the balcony after "ducking" into the theater? Now, he and Butch were guarding the fire exits in the orchestra, from where they could not see the front stairs coming down from the balcony, so the "funny" man, having seen two men looking around the balcony, could have run down the stairs and left the theatre. What kind of plan was that?

"Just before [the police] came, they turned the house lights on, and I looked out from the curtains and saw the man." "They" turned the lights on? Who was "they"? Julia was in the box office, so she wasn't "they." On a suspicion that a man acting "funny" who hadn't paid for a ticket was in the theatre? Stop the show? Before the police even get there? Why? Weren't "they" afraid this mad murderer would start shooting if "they" tried to apprehend him? And how did Johnny look out from the curtains if he was standing by the exit door and guarding it?

Another time check. At 1:30 Johnny sees the "funny" man in the shoe store lobby – for, say, two minutes – who then walks to the theatre, another two minutes, followed by Johnny, another two minutes, so it's at least 1:36 now. Johnny talks with Julia, goes in and talks with Butch, has to be three minutes, all told, so now it's 1:39. They check the exit doors, check the orchestra, go up to the balcony, look around, come down from the balcony, go out and tell Julia to call the police. How long did that take? At least five minutes? OK, 1:44. Julia supposedly calls the cops, while Johnny and Butch go to their fire exits to wait for the police, leaving the balcony and theater front entrances unguarded – anyone could have walked out. But, add one minute more, so 1:45 now. Johnny hears a noise outside, opens his door and sees the alley "filled with police cars." So, Julia called the cops at 1:44, and the cops all got there by 1:45. Amazing, don't you think?

New Orleans District Attorney Jim Garrison later said, "…at least thirty officers [including two captains, two FBI agents, and an assistant District Attorney] in a fleet of patrol cars descend on the movie theatre. This has to be the most remarkable example of police intuition since the Reichstag fire." Several of these policemen (including M. N. McDonald and Gerald L. Hill) came from the Tippit crime scene eight blocks away. How could they get there so fast?

Johnny Brewer went on: "[Oswald] stood up and walked to the aisle to his right and then turned around and walked back and sat down…. I heard a noise outside, and I opened the door, and the alley…was filled with police cars, and policemen were on the fire exits and stacked around the alley. And they grabbed me, a couple of them, and held and searched me and asked me what I was doing there, and I told them that there was a guy in the theatre that I was suspicious of, and he asked me if he was still there. And I said, yes, I just seen him. And he asked me if I would point him out. And I and two or three other officers walked out on the stage, and I pointed him out, and there were officers coming in from the front of the show, I guess, coming toward that way, and officers going from the back."

You can imagine what I'm thinking. The auditorium lights suddenly come on, but the film is still being projected onto the screen. That smells like trouble to me, so I get up and start to leave, when it strikes me: that's how I'll get killed, "trying to escape." So, I sit back down, and then a couple of cops and some guy come in through a fire exit by the screen, and the guy points in my direction. More cops, with shotguns, enter from the back. I know the headline, "Kennedy assassin attempts escape, is shot dead."

Keep in mind that *I didn't kill Officer Tippit*, wasn't at his murder scene, *didn't even know about his murder then*. I did fear I'd be killed somehow today, because I'm thinking, David Atlee Phillips has arranged for the Dallas cops to kill me if I try to run. So when the cops want to spook me by searching men near the front of the orchestra, I sit as still as a statue. "Oswald must've felt like Josef K in Kafka's *The Trial*," Jim Garrison later said.

Let me clear up a couple of things before I continue. First, I wasn't driven to the Texas Theatre just to get there quickly – it was to make sure the "patsy" was where he needed to be. Once I arrived, the guy who drove me there either radioed or telephoned that "the target is in place." That was no later than 1:15. Who was called next?

Second, why didn't Lee just go to ground, like every other shooter and associate? Because he was needed to impersonate me. Couldn't have been any other reason. Lee meeting Tippit was unfortunate for Tippit, who – desperate to find me – inadvertently ran into Lee. The plotters needed Lee to enter the theater, so that I could be killed there in a shootout with police, immediately closing the case. Nothing else makes sense. Otherwise, why was Lee *hurrying* – like at least one witness said – on East 10th Street in the direction of the Texas Theatre? Unless…he was *supposed* to meet and kill Tippit, go to the theatre, and have Tippit's murder blamed on me, as it actually was.

Here's what I think: the CIA advised the Dallas police that I would be in the Texas Theatre by 1:30. The "ducking into the theatre without paying for a ticket" ploy was the excuse, the cover story, for a platoon of cops to swoop down on the theatre a few minutes later. Don't ask me why Julia and Johnny went along with this fairytale – like I said, witnesses were pressured, witnesses were threatened, witnesses were killed.

In any case, this was supposed to be the final, successful, attempt to kill me. I was expected to "resist arrest," and be cut down in the alley by a dozen shotgun-wielding Dallas policemen. And, of course, I *supposedly* had "the revolver" that *supposedly* killed Tippet – *the one that had a bent firing pin, the one that didn't work, that couldn't shoot, that wasn't mine!*

As we come to my arrest, I have to tell you that from this point on you can't trust the statements and testimonies of the Dallas police and the FBI. Two reasons why: one, they *had* to provide 'evidence' to 'prove' I was a "lone nut" and a killer – anything else *had* to be changed, hidden, ignored, or destroyed; two, there *supposedly* were *no* tape recordings, stenographic records, or detailed notes by arresting officers and interrogators (during my trip to police headquarters, during the twelve hours of my interrogations, and when I was in my cell), so *any* words or actions could be laid on me once I was dead, with hardly any way to counter fabrications – especially since I was killed less than 48 hours later. The only quotes of *mine* you can really trust are what I told reporters in the halls, which were recorded. Anything else has to be examined, to see if it fits into the context of my life and this day – or not.

Let's take a quick look now at Dallas Police Officer C. F. Bentley Jr. He said he was in the neighborhood and heard a police radio dispatch that a suspect had entered the

Texas Theatre and *was in the balcony*. He parked out front, entered the theater with his shotgun, and was told "by a theater employee" that the suspect had gone *to the balcony*, so he and another officer quickly went up.

Only three to five people seemed to be there, but although the house lights were on it was still difficult to see. Just then C. F.'s uncle, Paul Bentley, a detective, accompanied by a second detective, came up, and Paul told C. F. to search everyone there and take their names. A moment later someone downstairs supposedly yelled, "The son of a bitch is downstairs!" And he and the other three officers turned and ran down the stairs, C. F. later told researcher Bill Drenas.

OK, now the *official* account of my arrest: one cop, M. N. McDonald, came to my row of seats and told me to stand up, which I did. I was in the fifth seat in, but he didn't report walking toward me. He told me to raise my hands, which I did, and, he testified, "I put my left hand on his waist and then his hand went to the waist. And this hand struck me between the eyes on the bridge of the nose." [Which fist did he hit you with?] "His *left fist*."

Officer C. T. Walker testified, "McDonald...was searching, and he felt of his pocket, and Oswald then hit him, it appeared, *with his left hand first, and then with his right hand.*" The same right hand that's also pulling out a gun? So, I had two right hands? I was right-handed, remember.

McDonald *said* I put my right hand on a pistol at my waist, *after* I hit him on his nose – and he put his left hand on my right hand. We both fell down between the rows of seats, me on top, and four other cops came and grabbed me, supposedly took a pistol from me, and handcuffed me. Everyone testified they heard the "click" of the trigger of a pistol being pulled, but later examination of 'my' pistol by an FBI technician showed no indentation, no trace, on any bullet, to indicate that the trigger had been pulled and the gun had misfired. Or, perhaps, since *I had no gun*, was that click McDonald's pistol, as he tried to kill me? Except that I grabbed the pistol, so that it couldn't discharge?

Officer McDonald told a different tale to *The Dallas Morning News*, which two days later quoted him as saying, "A man sitting near the front…tipped me the man I wanted was sitting in the third row from the rear, not in the balcony…. I went up the aisle, and talked to two people sitting about in the middle. I was crouching low and *holding my gun* in case any trouble came." If this was an accurate account, I'd have had to be suicidal to pull a gun on McDonald, and he would have been justified to immediately shoot me.

Then there was the account published in the November 23, 1963 issue of the *New York Herald Tribune*:

"It's all over now," said Lee Harvey Oswald softly....

"Police got a call that a man answering the description of the suspected assassin had entered the Texas Theatre. Patrolman J. D. Tippit and M. N. MacDonald followed. An usher told them the shabbily-dressed man had run into the theater.... They spotted the slim, balding, 5 foot nine-inch man crouched near a red-lighted exit door. They yelled.

"Patrolman Tippit fired once. Oswald fired once and Patrolman Tippit fell dead. Patrolman MacDonald then rushed and they struggled.... MacDonald was slashed several times across the face with a gun butt....

"As Patrolman MacDonald led the red-shirted suspect from the theater, a crowd of several hundred people milled about the entrance....

"Captain Gannaway said a Mauser rifle was found on a fifth floor landing of the [TSBD] building....

"His fellow employees speak of [Oswald] as being

'shabby' most of the time. They described his rather limp 'red' or 'brown' shirt and his rumpled trousers....

"Yesterday his brownish-colored jacket was found in a parking lot near the theater where he is accused of shooting Patrolman Tippit."

Wow! Which cop gave them *that* story?! I guess "limp" shirts and "rumpled" trousers are signs of a crazed assassin – but at least they got the color of my shirt half-right.

M. N. McDonald on November 22, 1963. My Marine Corps ring may have scratched the left side of his face. Slashed?

Let's see what other cops present in the theater testified. Motorcycle officer T. A. Hutson said, "I saw [Officer] McDonald down in the seat beside this person, and this person was in a half-standing crouching position, *pushing down on the left side of McDonald's face*, and McDonald was trying to push him off." ['This person was right-handed?... He was pushing on the left side of McDonald's face?'] "Right.... And McDonald was trying to hold him off with his hand.... I reached over from the back of the seat with my right arm and put it around this person's throat...and pulled him back up on the back of the seat that he was originally sitting in.

"At this time Officer C. T. Walker came up in the same row of seats that the struggle was taking place in and grabbed this person's left hand and held it. McDonald was at this time simultaneously trying to hold this person's right hand. Somehow this person moved his right hand to his waist, and I saw a revolver come out, and McDonald was holding on to it with his right hand, and this gun was waving up toward the back of the seat.... McDonald was using both of his hands to hold onto this person's right hand." What happened to the gun McDonald told the *Morning News* he had in his hand?

Detective Bob Carroll was asked, "['Who had hold of that pistol at that time?'] "I don't know, sir. I just saw the pistol pointing at me, and I grabbed it and jerked it away *from whoever had it*." Now, where did Bob Carroll come from? He had been at the TSBD, like Detective Jerry Hill.

So, one cop was holding tight to my left wrist, another had me pulled back off-balance against the back of my seat in a chokehold, a third cop was grabbing my right wrist, and somehow I *still* reached down to my waist, pulled out a handgun and was waving it toward the back seat – while the third cop held 'my' gun with his right hand and my right wrist *with both hands* (that makes two right hands on one cop), and a fourth cop pulled the gun from my right hand. Keep in mind that I weighed a whopping 132 pounds at this time and never worked out – a real monster. Does this account seem credible? The WC didn't care.

Besides Johnny Brewer, only two theater patrons testified for the WC – Julia testified she'd sold 24 tickets. Well, let's look at one of those testimonies, George Jefferson Applin's, since he supposedly was closest to me. At the time of my tussle with McDonald, George was standing three rows behind me, in the aisle to my right. "They came on up to Oswald, where he was sitting.... The officer said, "Will you stand up, please." ...When he stood up, the officer stepped over to search him down.... Oswald – or, the man – took a swing at him. When he did, the officer grabbed him." ['Took a swing at him with his fist?'] "Yes, sir; he did." ['With his left or right?'] "*Right fist....*"

The WC attorney went over the same ground again ['Then what did Oswald do?'] "He *took a right-hand* swing at him." ['Had you seen the pistol up to that time?'] "No, sir; there was not one in view then." ['How soon after that did you see the pistol?]' "I guess it was about 2 or 3 seconds." ['Who pulled the pistol?'] "*I guess it was Oswald, because – for one reason, that he had on a short sleeve shirt*, and I seen a man's arm that was connected to the gun." ['...any officers strike him?'] "I seen one strike him with a shotgun.... He grabbed the muzzle of the gun and drawed it back and swung and hit him in the back....with the butt end of the gun." ['...a hard blow?'] "Yes, sir."

Wait, three cops were holding me against the back of my seat – how could another one have hit me on my back with the butt of his shotgun? And, of course, I wasn't wearing a short-sleeved shirt – nor holding a pistol. So, although at least seven other young men in the orchestra had a clear view of McDonald and me when things went down, only one other was called by the WC – and his testimony was even less credible than Applin's. No one could ever talk to the rest of those men, since the police destroyed the witness list, probably because nothing claimed by the police actually happened, including when I got there.

Accident investigator Ray Hawkins was later asked, ['Did you see anybody strike Oswald during the struggle ...anybody strike him a blow?'] "No, sir, I did not see anyone strike him a blow." ['Afterwards, did you notice any marks on Oswald's face?'] "...Not at that time, but I did notice, however, after I saw him on television that he had a bruise on the right side of his face." ['Did you see that bruise there at the theater?'] "Not at the theater, no, sir." Well, one honest cop.

I twice shouted, "I am not resisting arrest," when I was being taken out. You know why. I also yelled, "I protest this police brutality." Why would I say that if I started the fight? Nothing said about me pulling a gun and trying to fire it, either by me or by the cops.

Why *wasn't* I charged with attempted homicide, if I'd pulled a gun and tried to fire it at a cop in the theatre? Prosecutors always pile on the charges. Why didn't any reporter ask me about drawing a gun? Why *would* I draw a gun? That'd be the best way to get killed. If I drew a gun and tried to fire it, why wasn't I shot? "Drawing a gun on an officer" seems like another part of the "Oswald Legend" – the 'mad killer' part, willing to kill anyone.

Consider the possibility that <u>I never had a handgun</u> with me in the theater, just as I never had a rifle at the TSBD. How could I have the handgun that killed Officer Tippit if I didn't kill him, wasn't there? Consider the possibility that McDonald had his gun out, was pointing it at me, was moving toward me, and I grabbed his gun with my left hand, since I expected to be shot, and pushed him backward, falling on him and scratching his face with my right hand.

Consider a further possibility: that some of the cops already knew I was in the theatre, their instructions were to kill me if I resisted (the platoon in the alley), so I was *protecting myself* from McDonald. The reason they didn't shoot me was because there were witnesses present in the orchestra, watching, who would have testified I didn't draw a pistol. Keep in mind that I was dead when the cops testified – they could say anything they wanted to – and only the two witnesses out of those sitting in the orchestra were ever identified or questioned.

In any case, the cops arrived by 1:45, they grabbed Johnny when he came out into the alley, frisked him, questioned him. Then a couple of cops went on the stage, and Johnny pointed me out, after which two men toward the front of the auditorium were checked out, patted down, and, finally, I'm approached, get into a scuffle, am subdued, handcuffed, and arrested. How long did all that take? Let's guess at least six minutes, so 1:51 P.M. The

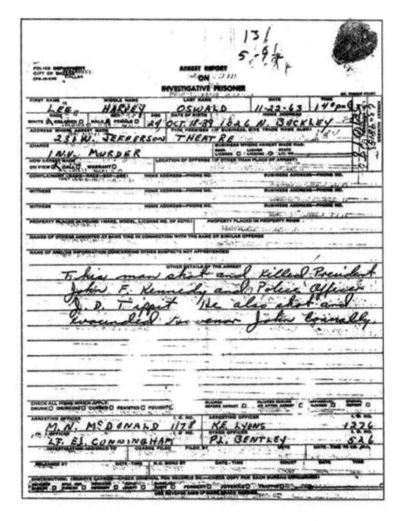

Dallas police arrest report, however, shows the time of my arrest to be 1:40 P.M. (above), so the Dallas police supposedly arrested me eleven minutes before they arrested me and five minutes before they got there. And see what they accuse me of, *with no proof*, an hour and ten minutes after JFK was killed.

What did the Dallas police *actually* have on me when I was arrested? I was just a man who worked at the TSBD, *who didn't fit Officer Baker's description, who couldn't have been* at 10th and Patton at 1:06 – or even at 1:10, who *wasn't dressed like Tippit's killer and had the wrong build and hair color,* and – if you've been following this tale carefully – *who wore a rust-brown tweed shirt all that day.* Really an airtight case – for my innocence!

Of course, I *supposedly* had a pistol – one that couldn't have been fired because it had a bent firing pin. I *supposedly* received 'my' pistol on March 20, 1963, so I *supposedly* would have had it eight months. Let me ask you: don't you think I would have test fired it at least once and discovered the bent firing pin? Has there ever been a man who bought a rifle or pistol and never test fired it? And how could I have killed Tippit with a gun like that?

Before I take you outside to the front of the theater, I want to jump ahead three or four minutes and keep looking inside the theater, because, years later, Butch Burroughs would give some jaw-dropping information to researcher James W. Douglas. Butch said he had seen *a second arrest* in the theater only three or four minutes after mine. The Dallas police had arrested a young man who "looked almost like Oswald, like he was his brother or something." Butch said he saw both me and him clearly, and that we looked alike. This is an important identification, because in the space of three or four minutes Butch had seen both of us and could easily compare Lee and me, revealing that Lee actually was not my "identical twin," just a lookalike.

Although I was taken out to the *front* of the theater, Lee was cuffed and taken out a *back* fire exit, into the alley. Standing in the alley watching was Bernard J. Haire, owner of Bernie's Hobby House, which was just two doors east of the theatre. He saw police bring out a flushed young white man dressed in slacks and a pullover shirt, put him in a squad car and drive off with him. It wasn't until 1987 that Mr. Haire discovered that the person he'd seen was *not* "Lee Harvey Oswald," not the man Jack Ruby shot.

There's verification of this in Dallas police records. The official Homicide Report on J. D. Tippit states, "Suspect was later arrested *in the balcony* of the Texas Theatre." In addition, Dallas Police Detective L. D. Stringfellow reported that, "Lee Harvey Oswald was arrested in the balcony of the Texas Theatre." That makes four separate reports about the *second* 'Lee Harvey Oswald,' Lee Oswald, being in the Texas Theatre.

A short time later, at about 2:00 P.M., T. F. White – a mechanic at Mack Pate's Garage, 114 7th Street, Oak Cliff, just over two blocks southwest of Beckley and Neely, eight blocks north of the Texas Theatre – saw a man he later said he believed was "Lee Harvey Oswald" drive into the parking lot of the El Chico restaurant across the street in a red 1961 Falcon, wearing a white T-shirt. Thinking the man was acting suspiciously, White took down the license plate number of the car, which was "PP 4537." Eventually, word got to the FBI, which checked and found that the license plate actually was issued to a blue 1957 Plymouth which belonged to Carl Amos Mather.

Mather was employed by Collins Radio, a major contractor with the CIA. During 1963 he had "serviced the communications gear aboard Lyndon Johnson's Air Force

Two," according to researcher Richard Gilbride. On November 22 Carl had returned home at 3:30 P.M. in his blue Plymouth. "While the wife was fairly calm, the husband was so 'upset' and 'agitated' that he was unable to eat." Mather was a communications expert, and it's believed there was radio communication between the assassins in Dealey Plaza and the plotters' nearby field headquarters. Someone had to have set up that equipment.

Surprisingly, the FBI sent agents to interview Mather, but he refused to speak with them, citing his high-security clearance. However, his wife Barbara *did* talk with agents, who she told that she and Carl *were close friends of J. D. Tippit and his wife Marie!* When Carl finally agreed to speak fifteen years later, with the HSCA – after he was granted immunity from prosecution – he could not explain how his license plate was seen on another car. As for what happened next to Lee Oswald, there's evidence he was flown out of Dallas on an Air Force C-54 the afternoon of the assassination.

So, the Dallas police department was playing a shell game, just like the CIA plotters. David Atlee Phillips missed his true calling: he should have been a screenwriter. What's still unknown, however, is how and *why* this second arrest, of Lee Oswald, came about. They'd already arrested 'Lee Harvey Oswald' a few minutes earlier.

The Patsy & "A. J. Hidell"

The cops then brought me outside. There was a virtual lynch mob before the theater. I was shoved into a police car, a detective sitting on either side of me. As we escaped from the crowd and drove toward police headquarters, another fairy tale began. The story is that supposedly one of the cops sitting next to me asked me for my name, and when I didn't answer him, he took my wallet from a pants pocket, looked through the wallet and found two IDs, one for "Lee Harvey Oswald," the other – a Selective Service card – for "Alek J. Hidell."

There were problems with this little tale, researcher Sylvia Meagher pointed out. The first and biggest was that no one at all – no policemen, no detectives, not the lead detective, not the chief of police, not an assistant D.A., not the D.A., not the FBI, not the Secret Service – ever spoke of "Alek J. Hidell " on this Friday. Mentioned was "O. H. Lee" and, of course, "Lee Harvey Oswald," but no "Alek J. Hidell." That's because the cops didn't receive the Hidell ID until Saturday, Ms. Meagher believed. And the *supposed* "Alek J. Hidell" ID at the Tippit murder scene? You'd think they would've shouted that to the rooftops! But no – silence covered it, like the cloak of night. Why?

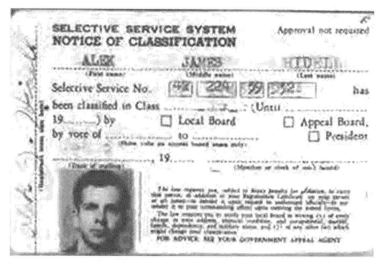

Once again, the photograph has the right half of Lee's face, the left half of mine, and not my chin. Compare this to the photo on p. 67.

Selective Service cards didn't have photographs on them. So, why did this phony one have one? To make it easier to identify me quickly. And where did that old photo with half Lee's face and half my face come from? The CIA. The card was made by the CIA, or FBI. One more anomaly: my wallet *supposedly* had an ID that read "Alek J. Hidell," and the WC noted that "the arresting officers found a forged selective service card with a picture of Oswald and the name 'Alek J. Hidell' in Oswald's billfold." The ID *supposedly* found in my arrest wallet, as you can see above, reads "Alek *James* Hidell," so could there have been two *different* ID cards? Remember that different configurations of this name were used for different code purposes. No Selective Service "Hidell" card was found in my wallet when I was arrested in New Orleans on August 9, although I was assumed to have forged the card at work in Dallas before I went to New Orleans.

The card appeared on Saturday to tie me to the forged order form for the Carcano rifle, which would tie me to the rifle, which *supposedly* would tie me to the murder of President Kennedy. All of it trying to frame me. And at that time in Texas I could have bought a rifle across the counter with *no* ID, and no one would have known I'd bought it.

So, why would I order a rifle by mail with a phony name?

Ten years later, ex-CIA agent and assassination researcher George O'Toole came across a recently invented investigative tool: Voice Stress Analysis (VSA), which could measure degrees of vocal stress caused by degrees of lying. The beauty of the technique was that the subject is not present for the analysis. Audio tapes – past and present – of the subject are fed into a device, the Psychological Stress Evaluator (PSE). An eighteen year study, published in 2013, found that VSA technology can identify emotional stress and detect lies better than a polygraph – it's 95% effective.

O'Toole was intrigued – he bought a PSE device, in 1973, and was trained to operate it. The degrees of stress using PSE were classified as "no stress," "moderate stress," "good stress," and "hard stress." So, "hard stress" is a barefaced lie. One of the first things to catch O'Toole's attention was 'my' "Alek J. Hidell" ID card.

O'Toole soon became interested in Detective Paul L. Bentley, who helped in arresting me and who sat to my left in the police car as I was taken to police headquarters. O'Toole (O) interviewed and audio taped Bentley (B) in 1973, analyzed his statements with PSE:

Detective Paul Bentley, center, cigar in his mouth, taking me out of the Texas Theatre, Sergeant Jerry Hill behind Bentley's left shoulder.

B. The gun was in his right hand.
Good to hard stress shown.

O. Which pocket was his wallet in?
B. Left rear pocket.
Hard stress shown.

O. ...he had both Hidell and Lee Harvey Oswald [IDs]?
B. There was three or four different names...in there.
Hard stress shown.

In a police report Bentley filed on December 3, 1963, he made only one reference to the wallet: "On the way to City Hall I removed the suspect's wallet and obtained his name." But even that's doubtful now.

When asked on TV if he was "familiar with this subject [Oswald]:"

B. No, I'd never seen him before.
Hardest stress shown.

Julia Postal later said that when I was taken out of the theater, officers arresting me identified me to her *by name* – Lee Harvey Oswald – and her statement is in a WC document.

Bentley's responses indicate that I had no handgun, that he didn't take my wallet from my pocket to check on my name, and that there was no Hidell card. And where had Bentley seen me before?

O'Toole also interviewed Police Sergeant Gerald "Jerry" L. Hill, who not only was present when 'my' rifle shells were 'found,' but who also showed up at the Tippit murder scene and was there when 'my' vanishing wallet was 'found,' was at the Texas Theatre and handled 'my' pistol, finally was in the police car with me and was party to the Hidell ID episode – present when almost every piece of phony 'evidence' against me was 'found.' Then he was interviewed on radio to talk about these 'finds.' Busy little bee. Does all this arouse anyone's curiosity?

Based on the research and analysis of Hasan Yusuf, a case can be made that Hill did do much to frame me. It seems he planted the Carcano shells on the sixth floor of the TSBD, then commandeered police car #207, drove to Beckley Avenue, picked me up at 1026, dropped me off at the Texas Theatre, then doubled back to the Tippit murder scene, handed 'my' phony wallet to Sergeant Croy (which could indicate that Tippit's murder was planned), returned to the Texas Theatre to plant 'my' pistol there, and finally sat in the police car with me and helped concoct the "Hidell ID" fable. Very plausible.

O'Toole noticed that although Hill told him my wallet had contained the Hidell card, Hill had made no mention of the Hidell name during the detailed radio interview he gave on the afternoon of November 22. Like researcher Sylvia Meagher, O'Toole questioned Hill's omission.

O'Toole fed a few of Hill's taped comments into his PSE device and later wrote that,

> A statement by Hill that "'We took his billfold out of his pocket' begins with virtually no stress but reaches good stress on the word 'pocket.' Stress reaches good to hard level during, 'we found the ID in both names, Oswald and Hidell,' and [good to hard level stress] remains there during, 'He had library cards and draft cards in one name, and he had identification cards from various organizations in the other name.'"

O'Toole also found *hard stress* on a tape of a CBS

interview with Hill, about the shells from the Carcano rifle 'found' at the TSBD.

Why were Bentley and Hill stressed about removing my wallet and cards from a back pocket, and why didn't Hill mention the Hidell card Friday? Easy. The cops didn't get the Hidell card from the CIA/FBI until Saturday, and they'd said nothing about it on Friday – because the CIA/FBI had told them nothing about "Hidell" on Friday – so the cops had to account for how they got their hands on the Hidell card. Like screenwriters, they had to create a "back story" to explain where the card had come from.

Someone made up the tale of me refusing to give my name in the car and Bentley *supposedly* reaching for my wallet and *supposedly* finding the Hidell card, along with my other cards. In reality, however, my wallet never left my pocket before I was booked – because Bentley and Hill already knew my name – and there was no "Hidell" card in my wallet. Which also means there was no "Hidell" card at the Tippit murder scene, either. Both stories are fiction, probably dreamed up by David Atlee Phillips.

Most likely the favored scenario of the plotters had been that the assassination was carried out by Cuban shooters sent by Fidel Castro, but – possibly as late as

Friday afternoon – the highest level of the cabal vetoed that story, believing it too dangerous. The fallback 'legend' was the "lone nut," but the materials for this weren't made available to the Dallas police on Friday. All of the errors relating to the 'guilt' of 'Lee Harvey Oswald' stem from that. After planning the ambush for more than a year, it's hard to understand why so many mistakes were made about 'Lee Harvey Oswald' if I'd been the chosen patsy all along.

A couple of things to finish the subject of 'my' names: First, at 3:15 P.M., November 22, the 112th Army Military Intelligence Group *supposedly* notified the FBI that I was using the name "Hidell." This, apparently, was *supposedly* after the Dallas police had called Lt. Colonel Robert Jones "advising that an A. J. Hidell" had been arrested in Dallas. Lt. Colonel Jones was an operations officer, and he *supposedly* quickly located the "Hidell" file, which was cross-referenced with another file on "Oswald." So, what was in the "Hidell" file – *if it ever existed*? No one knows. *Supposedly*, the WC never requested the file, and *supposedly* it was 'routinely' destroyed by the Pentagon in 1973. Incidentally, CIA agent Richard Case Nagell also used the "Alek Hidell" name, as researcher Dick Russell wrote.

Second, on the day of the assassination I was identified

"mistakenly" as "Harvey Lee Oswald" by the Dallas police and Army Intelligence. That name, reported assassination researcher Peter Dale Scott, was found more than two dozen times – starting in June, 1960 – in the files of the FBI, CIA, ONI, Secret Service, Dallas Police, Army Intelligence, and the Mexican Secret Police (DFS). So, obviously, no clerical error. Plus, New Orleans FBI agent John Quigley, speaking of my meeting with him in jail on August 10, 1963, told the WC, "...the jailer brought in an individual who was then introduced to me by Lieutenant Martello as Harvey Lee Oswald." Slip of the tongue? No. I

was "Harvey Lee" and Lee Oswald was "Lee Harvey" for intel identification.

Then there's the matter of 'my' pistol, which the WC claimed also was ordered by mail, January 27, 1963, by "A. J. Hidell," with another phony order coupon from some magazine (above), showing my age as 28. My fingerprints weren't on the coupon, of course. As with the Carcano, the pistol 'ordered' was different from the pistol 'sent.' And where did the six bullets in the pistol, the four rounds *supposedly* fired from it and the five loose rounds *supposedly* found in my pockets come from? No evidence of me buying boxes of bullets, no bullet boxes or other bullets found anywhere. Do you smell the odor of dead mackerel?

The Patsy & "A. J. Hidell"

Booked & Questioned

As I was taken into police headquarters, someone asked if I wanted my head covered. "Why should I hide my face," I told him, "I haven't done anything to be ashamed of." They then brought me to an interrogation room upstairs. "[Oswald] seemed quite calm, much calmer than I would have been," a detective later said. He asked me about shooting Tippit, and I replied, "I didn't shoot anybody!"

When Detective Captain Will Fritz learned who I was, I was moved to his office, and he started questioning me at 2:25. Eventually Fritz asked if I'd shot the president, and I told him, "No. I emphatically deny that." Then he asked if I'd shot Tippit. "No. I deny that, too," I replied. During the next two hours, I also was asked by an FBI agent if I'd been to Mexico City. How did the local FBI have intel about me being in Mexico within an hour and a half of arresting me? A "lone nut"?

By 3:00, FBI agents were fanning out across the country to talk with people who had known *me*, Harvey, and pick up every document relating to me: school records, work records, tax forms, military records, and so on, as well as some of Lee's records. How did they know where to go – especially where to look for *my* records? Back more than a dozen years? These records soon were either hidden in FBI files, altered and then photocopied, and/or destroyed. The WC received almost no original documents. The records of a "lone nut" are made to disappear? By mid-afternoon, the FBI had already located 'brother' Robert and was interviewing him, as well as Marina and Ruth Paine.

Will Fritz asked me where I was when the President was shot, and I told him outside the TSBD building, standing next to Bill Shelley. Saying that was a mistake, because the FBI got hold of the Altgens6 photo and removed Bill Shelley from beside me, and then everyone claimed that my figure was really Billy Lovelady.

At 4:30 P.M. I was taken for my first lineup. The lineups were all rigged. You may have noticed that Friday and Saturday I always was photographed wearing just a T-shirt and dark pants. Whatever happened to the rust-brown tweed shirt I was arrested in? After I was brought to police headquarters I was never again seen with that shirt on. Want to know why? Because the killer of J. D. Tippit was described as wearing dark pants and a light shirt under a jacket. No mention ever of a rust-brown tweed shirt that was hanging out. So, they couldn't put me in a lineup wearing a rust-brown shirt.

And the three men with me in the first lineup not only didn't look at all like me (they were larger and taller) but two had suits and ties and, of course, they didn't have bruises on their faces. I protested: "You are trying to railroad me…. You are doing me an injustice by putting me out there dressed different than these other men…. I am…the only one with a bruise on his head…. I don't believe the lineup is fair, and I desire to put on a jacket similar to those worn by some of the other individuals in the lineup. All of you have a shirt on, and I have a T-shirt on. I want a shirt or something…. This T-shirt is unfair…."

Later in the day they put three teenagers in another lineup with me. I protested again, "It isn't right to put me in line with these teenagers." At other lineups they brought in witnesses who had already seen me on television. Even then, a lot of witnesses couldn't identify me without nudging by the police. It was all a sham.

We returned to Fritz's office at 4:45, and he began questioning me again. I told him: "I want to talk with Mr.

Abt, a New York attorney.... I have not been given the opportunity to have counsel.... I never had a card to the Communist party.... I never ordered any guns." Then, dejectedly, "Everybody will know who I am now," meaning that my intelligence work would now be revealed.

Taken to my second lineup at 6:30, I shouted to reporters in the hall, "I didn't shoot anyone.... I never killed anybody." I was arraigned for the murder of Officer Tippit at 7:10. In the hall again at 7:50, I yelled, "I am only a patsy." Questioning was continued in Fritz's office at 8:00 by an FBI agent, and I told him, "I took a bus, but due to a traffic jam, I left the bus and got a taxicab, by which means I actually arrived at my residence." By this time I'd had enough, "I believe I've answered all the questions. I don't care to say anything else."

Wesley Frazier Again

An odd thing happened at 6:45 P.M. on November 22: Buell Wesley Frazier was arrested. That's right: arrested, the Randle home searched, and a .303 caliber British rifle with ammunition belonging to Frazier confiscated. *Why* this happened is still a mystery, but keep in mind that earlier that afternoon the Altgens6 photograph was being altered to black out the top of the TSBD the entryway.

That's not the end of the Frazier incident, though, for as he was being taken back to Irving at 9:00 P.M., the police driving him were radioed to return Frazier to Dallas police headquarters, where Captain Will Fritz asked him to take a lie detector test. That ended at 12:10 A.M., and Frazier *supposedly* passed it with flying colors. In how many books or articles do you see this whole event reported? Almost none. Routine, unimportant, you might say. It was anything but routine.

George O'Toole became very interested in Frazier, and began by analyzing a CBS recording of Frazier telling his

"Oswald curtain rods" story:

"PSE analysis of this [CBS] recording revealed a remarkable degree of stress throughout. It was such a classic example of the smooth, maximum hard stress waveform, maintained through almost the entire statement, that a PSE specialist to whom I showed it remarked, 'On a scale of ten, this stress is somewhere near eleven.' ...When Buell Wesley Frazier made that [CBS] statement, he was in a condition of sheer terror," O'Toole later wrote in his book.

Trying to find Frazier, O'Toole went to sister Linnie Mae's house, and "...she seemed to become increasingly tense...the color drained from her face" when she learned why O'Toole was there. She refused give Frazier's address to O'Toole, said Frazier was in the Army.

O'Toole spoke with Dallas detectives once more. When he asked Paul Bentley – senior polygraph examiner for the Dallas police – about Frazier's polygraph exam, Bentley replied, "I don't recall that even occurring," which statement brought forth *maximum hard stress*. When Detective R. D. Lewis was asked if he'd tested Frazier, he said, "No, I don't remember giving anybody one," eliciting *hard stress*. Isn't that interesting – two veteran Dallas police polygraph experts nailed by VSA ten years later.

When Jerry Hill said Captain Fritz didn't believe in polygraphs, so didn't use them, *near-maximum stress* appeared. Detective Richard Stovall vaguely recalled a Frazier exam, but when asked if only Frazier and the examiner were present replied, "Well, as far as I know," eliciting *hard stress*. Detective Guy Rose said, "There was only one officer in the room with him" and "…[Frazier] was telling just exactly the truth," which statement resulted in *hard stress*. Why were *five detectives* lying about the polygraph exam? Jim Bishop wrote that there were five police officers in the room during the polygraph exam and that Frazier's responses "bordered on controlled hysteria."

O'Toole found a man, in 1973 – formerly with both the FBI and the CIA – to locate where Frazier was, but the man's FBI contact emphatically refused any information – Frazier's file was "red tagged," which meant the FBI was still keeping an eye on him ten years later. Why, if he was just an ordinary witness? But O'Toole finally got lucky, hiring private investigator Anthony Pellicano, who found Wesley Frazier (F) in forty-eight hours and taped a phone interview with him, which *both* O'Toole and Pellicano analyzed, separately, with PSE. Here are the highlights of

Frazier's statements, with results:

F. "Lee" wanted to go get curtain rods Thursday afternoon:
Maximum hard stress.

F. More about "Lee" and the curtain rods:
Nearly maximum hard stress.

F. "Lee" took the package into the TSBD:
Maximum hard stress.

F. Only the polygraph operator was in the room with Frazier:
Maximum hard stress.

F. He passed the polygraph test and did well:
Maximum hard stress.

F. He didn't know who Paul Bentley was:
Maximum hard stress.

Fifty years later a journalist interviewed Frazier and wrote:

"Police arrested Frazier as a suspected accomplice of Oswald's.... He was fingerprinted, photographed and forced to take a lie detector test. 'I was interrogated and questioned for many, many hours,' Frazier said. 'Interrogators would rotate.' Dallas police Capt. Will Fritz, who was in charge of the homicide department, came into the room with a typed statement. He handed Frazier a pen and demanded he sign it. It was a confession. Frazier refused. 'Captain Fritz got very red-faced, and he put up his hand to hit me, and I put my arm up to block. I told him we'd have a hell of a fight, and I would get some good licks in on him. Then he stormed out the door.' ...At around 3 A.M. the next day, police let Frazier go."

So, what was the whole Frazier thing about? Have to conclude he was threatened to say what he later did or be accused of being my accomplice – or worse. Poor Wesley. Watched and terrorized for dozens of years, still telling the same tale – but still alive at seventy-one.

Arraigned

Still Friday, just before 9:00 P.M., they fingerprinted me and did a paraffin test on my hands and cheek. I told them, "What are you trying to prove with this paraffin test, that I fired a gun? You are wasting your time. I don't know anything about what you are accusing me." They found no gunpowder residue on my cheek, and although nitrates were found or my hands, nitrates are found in ink, which was on boxes I'd handled for four hours that morning.

I tried to make a long distance call shortly before 10:45 P.M. but was told it didn't go through, which was a lie. Here's what happened: the two police phone operators on duty – Alveeta Treon and Louise Swinney – were told that two lawmen would soon come to listen in on a call I'd be making. The men arrived, showed their credentials, and went into a room next to the switchboard. Around 10:45 a red light blinked on the telephone panel, showing I had picked up the handset in the jail phone booth.

Swinney alerted the two agents and handled the call, as

Treon listened in on line and wrote down on a message slip what I said. I asked to call a John Hurt collect, and I gave Swinney two North Carolina numbers. She wrote these down and began to put the call through to the first number. "I was dumbfounded at what happened next," Mrs. Treon later said. "Mrs. Swinney opened the key to Oswald and told him, 'I'm sorry, the number doesn't answer.' She then unplugged and disconnected Oswald without ever trying to put the call through. A few moments later Mrs. Swinney tore the page off her notation pad and threw it into the wastepaper basket."

Treon kept the slip with the notes she had written on it as a souvenir. Researchers later found that the numbers were for two Raleigh men – John D. Hurt and John W. Hurt – both of whom denied knowing about "Lee Harvey Oswald" and his attempted phone call, but one of the men, John David Hurt, served in U.S. military counter intelligence during World War II. And we've all learned there's no such thing as a "former" intelligence officer, right?

Some researchers feel that John David Hurt may have been a military intelligence "cut-out," someone who'd pass on an agent's seemingly innocuous message to an intelligence handler, without the "cut-out" knowing who the agent was or what the agent might be involved in, insulating the "cut-out" from any criminal act and creating space between the agent and his handler, allowing for "plausible deniability."

But the call was a mistake on my part – an intelligence operative later told a researcher that I would have been killed for just attempting the call, since that was a lead that could have exposed the entire plot if it had been properly investigated. Neither the WC nor the HSCA investigated this event. Eventually, researcher Sherman Skolnick got hold of a photocopy of the phone slip.

HSCA Chief Counsel G. Robert Blakey in 1979 told researcher Anthony Summers, "It was an outgoing call, and therefore I consider it very troublesome material. The direction in which it went was deeply disturbing."

At 11:26 P.M. I was arraigned for the murder of President Kennedy, then was taken to a news conference. A newsman asked, "Did you kill the President?" I told him, "No.... I did not do it. I did not do it – I did not shoot anyone." Jack Ruby was somehow in the back of the room, and, he later said, had his pistol in his pocket.

Doppelgänger: The Legend Of Lee Harvey Oswald

Backyard Photo

The next morning, at 10:30, I was again interrogated in Capt. Fritz's office, where I told him, "I am familiar with all types of questioning and have no intention of making any statements.... I didn't tell Wesley Frazier anything about bringing back some curtain rods.... I did carry a package to the Texas School Book Depository – I carried my lunch, a cheese sandwich and fruit, which I made at Paine's house." Remember that there was no stenographer present, nor was a tape recorder used, at any of my interrogations, so these statements are what others said they recalled or wrote in brief notes. But, again, notice my stiff and foreign-sounding language.

At 1:15 P.M. I spoke with Marina and my 'mother,' and at 2:15 another rigged lineup was held with me in my T-shirt again. At 3:30 'brother' Robert came. He obviously was in a quandary: he'd only signed up to help a CIA agent and now was an inadvertent party to an assassination. Of course, he had no idea if I was involved or not – he hadn't seen me for a year. I told him, "I don't know what is going on. I just don't know what they are talking about.... Don't believe all the so-called evidence." When he looked into my eyes for a clue, I said to him, "Brother, you won't find anything there."

At 6:25 I was again talking with Will Fritz. He showed me the "backyard" photograph, in which 'I' was holding 'my' pistol, 'my' rifle, and copies of *The Militant* and *The*

Worker in the backyard of 214 W. Neely Street. I told him the photo was fake, a forgery. First of all, there's something wrong with the head – seems to be more in focus than the rest of the picture, too big for the body under it, and not set right on the neck.

Then, the shadows on my face go straight down, but the shadow behind me angles to my right. And when you enlarge the picture, you can see that the chin isn't mine –

My chin. *Not my chin!*

it's square, not pointed, with no cleft – and you can see where my face is attached at the chin. Look at the right arm and hand, too – they belong to a man larger than me – plus the tips of the fingers seem to be missing. I told Fritz that the upper part of my face had been glued onto the picture, and I'd be able to prove that. Three different versions of the photograph eventually turned up, and researchers later showed other things wrong with it. Police photographer Roscoe White is suspected of helping to fabricate the photo, possibly posing for it.

Last, but not least, was the Imperial Reflex camera *supposedly* used by Marina to take the backyard photos. It wasn't among my things at my rooming house; it wasn't found at Ruth Paine's house; and Marina first described a very different camera she said she used to take the photos. 'My' Imperial Reflex camera first surfaced *three months* after November 22, on February 14, 1964 *when 'brother' Robert gave it to the FBI*. So, where did Robert – who lived in Fort Worth – get the camera? *Supposedly* from Ruth Paine, who lived in Irving and repeatedly came up with evidence to frame me in the months after the assassination, long after the police had gone over her house and garage with a fine-tooth comb. And why would Ruth call Robert, who she barely knew?

I also twice told Fritz that I'd *never lived on Neely Street*, plus I didn't include Neely Street on a list of prior addresses that I provided to an FBI agent. Here's what this was all about: the CIA/FBI wanted to incriminate me with

Backyard Photo

212-214 W. Neely Street.

212-214 back yard.

the "backyard photo." For that, they needed a back yard for the picture, one that was somewhat secluded. The Elsbeth apartments had no such back yard, but 212-214 W. Neely Street, apparently another CIA "safe house," did have a suitable yard.

The WC claimed that I, Marina and June had lived upstairs and that another couple had lived downstairs. Before I refute that, notice that there's no house next door at the left, nor does there seem to be one at the right, so no nosy neighbors. The back yard also seems to be secluded, perfect for shooting the phony "backyard photo." A 1963 document notes that "there are no other houses facing on Neely Street in the block where this residence is located." So, this structure was somewhat isolated, ideal for a "safe house."

The only 'evidence' to 'prove' that I lived at 214 W. Neely for seven weeks is an affidavit dated *June 12, 1964*, in which an M. Waldo George, claiming to be office manager of the Tucker Manning Insurance Company of Dallas, stated that he owns the Neely Street duplex and rented the upper floor to me on March 2, 1963.

Problems with the affidavit: 1) there are no rent receipts or any other records, 2) the FBI submitted no utility or phone bills for that address, 3) Waldo George also was listed in WC documents under the names F. M. George and Jim W. George, 4) no researcher is known to have found and interviewed George, 5) 202 days went by before George's sworn affidavit supposedly was taken, and 6) nearby neighbors had never seen me and my family.

George and his wife didn't testify for the WC. Why? The Elsbeth apartment managers, Mahlon Tobias and his wife, *did* testify, on April 2, 1964, Mahlon saying, "I have been goofy-headed all of my life." Landlady Mary Bledsoe testified, on April 2, as did housekeeper Earlene Roberts, on April 8, and Dallas YMCA desk clerk Colin Barnhorst, on April 1, along with my New Orleans landlady, Jesse Garner, on April 6. The Georges were my only Dallas landlords not called to testify, and Waldo's affidavit *(supposedly)* was taken in June, rather than early April, when all the others testified.

Waldo George also stated in the affidavit that the downstairs unit was occupied by Mr. and Mrs. George B. Gray, who were never interviewed by the FBI and who have never been found by researchers. George said on November 29, 1963, that the Grays occupied 212 W. Neely from February 16 to May 1 but that he "believed they had left Dallas...and he had no idea how to locate [them]." To add insult to injury, George said that the Grays had *supposedly* called him to complain that "the man in the upstairs apartment was beating his wife." But wait! Did the Grays have a phone? They weren't listed in the 1963 Dallas telephone directory. And when Marina was asked by the WC if there was "any violence or any hitting of you? Did that occur on Neely Street?" Marina replied, "No, that was on Elsbeth Street." This *supposed* 'report' by the Grays was part of my demonization – 'the vicious husband.'

The supposed existence of the Grays is anchored completely in M. Waldo George's affidavit and other statements. The Dallas City Directory of 1963 listed the 214 W. Neely Street apartment as vacant in 1962 and Lillie Hoover (supposedly the owner of the property that year but never found by researchers) as living in the downstairs apartment at 212 W. Neely. The 1964 Dallas City Directory listed both Neely apartments as empty in 1963.

In another statement on November 29, George said "he was in error" that the Oswalds had resided at 214 W. Neely Street from April 1 to May 31, 1963, now saying the dates were from March 2 to May 1. That change was needed by the WC, obviously, because I left Dallas for New Orleans on April 25. However, Mr. and Mrs. Marvin Friddle, 702 N. Madison Avenue, on November 29, 1963, told the FBI they didn't know the Oswalds but "do know that a young man, his wife, and *two small children* had resided at the upstairs apartment [214 Neely]…for a very short time, around April and May – they would see him, his wife and *children* around the house and on the upstairs balcony."

So, nothing is known about Mr. and Mrs. George B. Gray – or even that there ever was a George B. Gray, and there's nothing to show that the content of M. Waldo George's affidavit has any truth to it.

Here's the completely bogus tale the WC wanted you to believe:

> In late January, I filled out a form to order a mail-order revolver, and the coupon was supposedly received by Seaport Traders on March 13. At the beginning of March, I supposedly was asked to leave our Elspeth apartment because tenants had complained I was drinking, yelling and beating Marina. We immediately moved to West Neely Street on March 3. The next weekend, March 9-10, I reconnoitered the home of former General Edwin Walker, 4011 Turtle Creek Blvd, Dallas (6.6 miles

north of Neely Street, reached by a complex route), and photographed his house – the picture later 'found' in Ruth Paine's magical garage, which on command could crank out any needed 'evidence' against me. (Unknown when and where the film was developed, and what and where the other pictures on the roll were.)

On March 12, I mail-ordered a Carcano rifle, and on March 25 I went to the downtown post office after work and picked up a 40" rifle (having ordered a 36" rifle), of which there never was a record at the P.O. How did I know the rifle had arrived? I went home on a bus, but no one saw me with the package. I got off the bus, but no one saw me walk home. When I got home, Marina did not see the package, nor did she see me unwrap the rifle, nor see the box or packing material it had been shipped in. I made no complaint to the seller about getting the wrong rifle.

In the same time frame, I 'received' the wrong revolver – I ordered a $29.95 revolver but got a $39.95 revolver instead, sent by American Express – of which there also was no record.

Backyard Photo

On March 31 – a cloudy and rainy day – Marina photographed 'me' in the Neely back yard, proudly holding the rifle and two newspapers, the revolver in a holster on 'my' hip, like a kid who got a cap pistol and a BB rifle for Christmas. No one knows where 'my' holster came from, or when. Marina said she took the pictures "towards the end of February, possibly the beginning of March" – although I *supposedly* got the guns March 25.

On April 10, I came home, ate dinner, then took the rifle out of the house with me, without Marina seeing me, walked down the street to a bus stop, rode one or more busses to General Walker's neighborhood, set up my shot without being seen, fired one round into his home at 9 P.M., and then – still no one seeing me – "ran several kilometers [holding the rifle in my hands?] and then took the bus," Marina testified. On the way home I buried the rifle somewhere, she said I told her.

Isn't that a charming tale? Nothing but lies.

In addition, Marina falsely testified not only that we'd moved to Neely Street, "In January, after the new year," but that she'd seen 'my' rifle (which she said had no scope) for the first time at Neely Street, "I think that was in February," "standing up in a corner or on a shelf," that she'd observed me cleaning 'my' rifle "four or five times" (although no cleaning equipment or supplies were ever found), that she'd also seen 'my' rifle for "the first time in New Orleans" (making that the *second* "first time" she'd seen it), that she'd seen boxes of ammunition (both at Neely Street and in New Orleans), and that she'd stopped me from killing Richard Nixon. She also "recognized" 'my' revolver and its holster. The WC believed that I practiced using 'my' rifle, although I had no car and no one ever saw either me or 'my' rifle. And, sure enough, Marina claimed I'd told her I was going out to practice with 'my' rifle.

The only rational conclusion to reach about all this is that *we never lived at the Neely Street duplex*, which was a CIA "safe house" that just served as the backdrop for the "backyard photo." So, not only was that photo phony but my supposed seven week stay with Marina and June at 214 W. Neely Street and *everything* that supposedly happened there is *complete* fiction, quite likely authored by the CIA's playwright and master of disinformation, David Atlee Phillips. And if the photo is fraudulent, then everything alleged about 'my' rifle and revolver is also false and proves I was framed.

I finally told Capt. Fritz, "*The only thing I am here for is because I popped a policeman in the nose* in the theater on Jefferson Avenue, which I readily admit I did, *because I was protecting myself*.... I never ordered any rifle by mail order or bought any money order...for such a rifle.... I didn't own any rifle. I have not practiced or shot with a rifle since I was in the Marine Corps." Notice that I said *nothing* about a revolver.

After forty-five minutes, Fritz tossed in the towel, concluding I was either "the victim of an immense and well-coordinated conspiracy," or "a psychopathic liar." I was then taken through the third floor hallway, where a reporter shouted, "Did you fire that rifle?" To which I replied, "I don't know what dispatches you people have been given, but I emphatically deny these charges.... I have not committed any acts of violence." Again, that language is not what a tenth grade dropout raised in New Orleans would use.

Doppelgänger: The Legend Of Lee Harvey Oswald

Execution & Funeral

The next morning, November 24, at 9:30 A.M., Fritz started questioning me again and asked about the "A. J. Hidell" ID he said was found in my wallet. Now I knew for certain I was being set up – that card hadn't been in my wallet. Someone had given that to the Dallas police. Postal Inspector Harry Holmes testified, "That is the only time that I recall [Oswald] kind of flared up, and he said [to Fritz], 'You know as much about it as I do.' And he showed a little anger. Really the only time that he flared up." You bet I was mad – David Atlee Phillips and his boys were framing me. Even a dead man would have been angry.

However, several detectives later talked about how well I'd held up during questioning, "He conducted himself better than anyone I have ever seen during investigation." "I never saw a man that could answer questions like he did." "Oswald knew exactly when to talk and when to stop." "He was way ahead of everybody else – he knew what he was doing and seemed very confident." "He acted like he was in charge, and, as it turned out, he probably was." Fritz wondered whether I had received special training in how to deflect police questioning. I certainly had.

About 11:00 A.M., as I was getting ready to be transferred to the county jail, Detective James Leavelle put one end of handcuffs on his left wrist, the other on my right wrist, and jokingly said to me, "Lee, if anybody shoots you, I hope they're as good a shot as you are," to which I supposedly replied, "You're just being melodramatic."

We went downstairs and entered the underground garage at 11:21. A reporter shouted at me, "Do you have anything to say in your defense?" Before I could respond, Jack Ruby lunged out of the crowd of reporters, yelling, "You killed my president, you rat son of a bitch!" and pulled the trigger of a handgun, shooting me in my left side, the bullet passing through every major organ in my abdomen and cutting through my aorta.

Why did Jack Ruby shoot me? He had to. I was supposed to have been killed on November 22 but somehow wasn't. That was a *big* problem for the plotters – they couldn't have withstood an investigation and trial by any competent defense lawyer. Ruby had to eliminate me.

Execution & Funeral

He was the only plotter with easy access to police headquarters, where he knew everyone and regularly brought the cops sandwiches, including this weekend. Jack was told that if he didn't kill me, the Mob would not only kill him but his brothers and sisters as well. Poor Jack had no choice. He knew they'd do it, and he knew his own death wouldn't be pretty if he didn't carry out this hit.

After I was taken to the jail office, a medical student named Beiberdorf, working in the jail that day, gave me CPR, the worst thing to do for a person with a gunshot wound to the abdomen, because pushing down on the chest just pumps more blood out of the body. He kept doing CPR until the ambulance arrived, three to five minutes after I was shot.

The ambulance drove me to Parkland Hospital, where JFK had been taken. Beiberdorf came with me and not only continued to work on my chest but also placed an oxygen cup resuscitator over my mouth – which can be fatal to a victim with a gunshot wound to the stomach. When we arrived, doctors worked feverishly to try to save my life. They got me stabilized briefly, but then, after immense blood loss, my heart failed and couldn't be started again.

I died at 1:07 P.M., at the age of 23. The plotters had

their execution. Now my demonization would begin.

On the gloomy afternoon of November 25, just after 4:00 P.M., my body was driven for burial to a remote corner of Rose Hill Cemetery in Fort Worth. Every church and every pastor approached had refused to conduct a service for me. One minister finally agreed to come to the burial but didn't show up. The executive secretary of the Fort Worth Council of Churches finally came to say a few words.

Only Marina, June, Rachel, Robert and 'Marguerite' attended the burial. There were no pallbearers: reporters present had to volunteer to carry my coffin. The whole thing lasted twenty minutes. The coffin was lowered into the ground at 4:28.

I no longer had to play the role of 'Lee Harvey Oswald.'

Aftermath

What happened to Lee Oswald? There were three possibilities: 1) he was flown out of the country, never to return, 2) he was given a new identity and pension, and 3) he was 'eliminated.' All three required his disappearance. The third option is most likely, since the plotters couldn't take any chances, and there's evidence that this is what happened.

Dallas morticians Paul Groody and Alan Baumgardner had prepared my body for burial in 1963, embalming it with several times the usual amount of formaldehyde, should my body ever be needed in the future. They then placed the body in a wood casket, which was put in a 2700 pound vault made of steel-reinforced heavy concrete with an asphalt lining – guaranteed not to break, crack, or go to pieces. The casket and vault were both hermetically sealed.

When the vault was exhumed in 1981, Groody and Baumgardner were present and saw that its bottom was now broken, although the top was still intact. However, the casket's top – just above and behind the head – also was damaged, with a section *missing*. Human remains could be seen through the large hole, but since water and air had entered over the years, only the skull and skeleton remained. The morticians next noticed the *lack of a craniotomy* – when the skull cap is cut off to remove the brain during an autopsy – *which <u>had</u> been done* to my head during my autopsy.

Four forensic pathologists compared the teeth in the skull with 'Lee Harvey Oswald's' Marine Corps dental records (but *which* 'Oswald' records?), noted a hole caused by a mastoidectomy on the left side of the skull (but there's no picture of it), and concluded, "Beyond any doubt, and I mean any doubt, the individual buried under the name Lee Harvey Oswald...is in fact Lee Harvey Oswald." Again, which one? Remember, I never had a mastoidectomy. If it *was* Lee, then either our bodies were switched or he and I literally were merged in death, his skull and my skeleton – only the heads exchanged, probably in 1964.

Groody provided an explanation, "I feel as though someone had gone to the cemetery [during]...off hours, had taken the head of Lee Harvey Oswald, brought the vault to the surface as best they could, being a heavy item.... The

Aftermath

vault fell, breaking [it], causing the casket to deteriorate to a degree. Then, of course, removed the head of the one that was there that had been autopsied, and put this head in its place so that we would find the teeth of Lee Harvey Oswald.... Whoever caused that is the same faction that caused the assassination in the first place. In my mind, a cover-up had taken place." So Lee may have met the same fate I did.

What about Marina? On February 3, 1964, she testified before the WC, lying as well as any CIA agent, especially about 'my' rifle and about the "backyard photograph" she said *she* took of 'me.' Can't blame her, though – after all, she was a twenty-two-year-old recent Russian immigrant, a

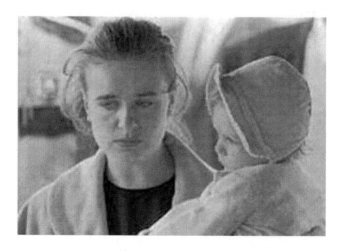

widow with two babies, broke, no job and no income, who was terrified of being sent back to Russia or imprisoned here, and who was 'interviewed' at least forty-six times in the previous seventy-three days by the FBI and the Secret Service – what would you have done? She joined the charade and parroted the 'facts' the FBI had taught her.

Five days later, on February 8, a 'movie production company' rented a small office on the Samuel Goldwyn Studios lot in Los Angeles. The company was called Onajet Productions, also known as Tex-Italia Films and Cinema International Productions. Note the first name: "On-a-jet."

On February 15, Marina signed a contract with Onajet and was paid a large but odd amount: $132,350 – $75,000 for worldwide movie and TV rights, $7,500 for each film appearance, and $1,500 for each personal appearance. $132,350 in 1963 is roughly equal to $1,000,000 in 2016.

So, a 'movie production company' that has no previous history pays Marina the equivalent of a million 2016 dollars, never makes a film, never has Marina appear on TV or make a personal appearance, is shortly kicked off the Goldwyn lot *for not paying its office rent*, and then the Onajet 'producers' – who gave phony names – get "on a jet," disappear and are never heard of again, without even trying to sell the rights they 'bought' from Marina. And who let them on the Goldwyn lot, anyway?

You know as well as I do where the money came from: the CIA. I was a full-time field agent of the Agency, but most of my salary wasn't paid out to me during my time of service. I figure at least $50,000 given to Marina was a death benefit; the rest was the pay for my years with the Agency – plus something for Marina's 'cooperation' and silence, from the Agency funds allocated to the "Oswald Project," pocket change for the Agency.

Who else would've done this? Those three CIA guys must have enjoyed playing "The Producers." If all this hadn't been so vicious, traitorous and tragic, it would've been hilarious: a "B" movie, a slapstick farce with the Keystone Cops, and Laurel and Hardy playing Lyndon Johnson and J. Edgar Hoover.

On March 22, 1978, James B. Wilcott, a former CIA paymaster, testified before the HSCA that he believed I had been a full-time field agent for the CIA, working in the "Oswald Project," given a full-time salary for doing CIA operational work as an agent, for which project Wilcott believed he had disbursed funds in Japan. And remember that 'cousin' Marilyn had "facilitated" that project as a CIA operative while in Japan.

In 1996 former Deputy Counsel for the HSCA Robert

Tanenbaum testified at the *Assassination Records Review Board* hearing in Los Angeles that in 1964 Texas Attorney General [Waggoner Carr], Dallas District Attorney Henry Wade, and attorney Leon Jaworsky spoke to Chief Justice [Earl Warren] "and said in substance that they had information from unimpeachable sources that Lee Harvey Oswald was a contract employee of the CIA and the FBI." Warren said he'd look into that. There's no record he ever did.

So, were James Wilcott, Robert Tanenbaum, Waggoner Carr, Henry Wade, and Leon Jaworsky all lying? Not likely – none of them had anything to gain, but had a lot to lose, including their reputations and lives.

Others who looked into the assassination came away believing there had been a conspiracy. Early in '64, WC member Senator Richard Russell asked Army Intelligence Col. Phillip Corso to quietly investigate "Oswald." Corso reported back that two U.S. passports had been issued to "Lee Harvey Oswald," which had been used by two different men. Corso also discovered – from William C. Sullivan, head of the FBI's Domestic Intelligence Division – that there were two different birth certificates for "Lee Harvey Oswald," also used by two different men. Russell and Corso concluded there'd been a conspiracy.

Republican Senator Richard Schweiker told researcher Anthony Summers, "...one of the biggest cover-ups in the history of our country occurred.... Oswald was playing an intelligence role.... [He was] a product of, and interacting with, the intelligence community." Summers also quoted an unnamed HSCA staff investigator, "In the months leading up to the assassination, I think Oswald got in over his head. He was no longer quite sure who he was working for, or why. Somebody was using him, and they knew exactly how and why."

Jim Garrison wrote, "[Oswald] was employed by the Central Intelligence Agency and was obviously drawn into a scapegoat situation and made to believe ultimately that he was penetrating the assassination. And then when the time came, they took the scapegoat – the man who thought he was working for the United States government – and killed him real quick. And then the machinery, disinformation machinery, started turning, and they started making a villain out of a man who genuinely was probably a hero."

Richard Case Nagell said about me, "If I was mountain climbing, I would trust that guy to hold the end of my rope in a crisis. He had a lot of control over himself. He was articulate, though you'd never get that impression from reading what he's written, because his spelling was atrocious. He could hold a good conversation on just about anything political. He was cautious. He was no crazier than the rest of us."

George de Mohrenschildt stated, "No matter what they say, Lee Harvey Oswald was a delightful guy. They make a moron out of him, but he was smart as hell. Ahead of his time really, a kind of hippie of those days. In fact, he was the most honest man I knew. And I will tell you this: I am sure he did not shoot the president." Both George and his wife later insisted to Jim Garrison that I'd just been the scapegoat of the assassination.

George O'Toole gets the last word with his PSE analysis of my core statement, which was recorded in a Dallas Police Headquarters corridor:

Reporter: Did you shoot the president?

Harvey: I didn't shoot anybody, no sir.

Here's what O'Toole wrote after his PSE analysis of that statement: "His categorical denial that he shot anyone contained almost no stress at all…. Lee Harvey Oswald was telling the truth."

O'Toole wanted a second opinion, so he got a "former

army intelligence agent and one of the most experienced polygraph examiners in the country," Lloyd H. "Rusty" Hitchcock, to also run a PSE test on my statement. Hitchcock wrote, "I can state, beyond reasonable doubt, that Lee Harvey Oswald did not kill President Kennedy and did not shoot anyone else." O'Toole asked several other experts to run PSE analyses of my statement as well, and they all reached the same conclusion: I was innocent.

Case closed.

All the lies about me aren't important to *me* any longer, because where I am all lies and all truth are known by everyone. But my story *is* important to *you*, because you need to learn about those lies and the ones about JFK's assassination, and you need to know who was responsible, so that this country can finally exit the hideous nightmare of JFK's assassination and my execution and cleanse the soul of the United States of America of this moral cancer. My story is only a small part of the whole picture, but once you realize I wasn't "a lone nut" and didn't murder JFK, you'll be freed to demand the truth from your government.

Thanks for listening to me. Good hunting for the truth.

'Harvey Oswald'

"The president was killed by a person or persons unknown. Until the murderers are found, until the truth is known, until justice is done, there can be no rest and no peace. None for John Kennedy, none for Lee Oswald, and none for the rest of us."

George O'Toole, 1975

Afterword

"If the American people knew the truth about Dallas, there would be blood in the streets."

Robert F. Kennedy

So, what was this moral and political upheaval all about? Simply put, control of the presidency. It was no coincidence that Lyndon Johnson was in that fateful motorcade. The plotters wanted him to know that he, also, was at their mercy. As for the spooks, generals, Cuban exiles and the Mob, the assassination was a deception provocation intended to facilitate a U.S. military invasion of Cuba.

It was a multi-faceted plan dreamed up by David Atlee Phillips and likely James Jesus Angleton, along with a few of their top-echelon CIA buddies. Think of a quintuple fish hook, having five barbs, each of which has a different piece of delicious bait stuck on it. Depending on what attracts a certain fish, different fish will bite on different bait. So here are the five baits (scenarios) on the barbs of the plotters:

1. The "lone nut" bait. According to the CIA and FBI, all political assassins have been "lone nuts," if you're willing to swallow that. This particular "lone nut" admired Russia and Castro, felt Kennedy was disrespecting them.

Personnel: Supposedly one "lone nut" patsy, whose 'legend' has been designed over the previous six years to be someone every American can loathe. Once JFK is dead, he is killed 'resisting arrest.'

2. The "Castro" bait. Castro – America's "commie" boogie man of South America – supposedly finds out that the Kennedys want to assassinate *him*, so he decides to turn the tables and kill JFK.

Personnel: Supposedly the "lone nut," who loves Castro, of course, but if any Cuban exile plotters are also caught, the CIA can say they were actually Castro operatives, so it all falls on Castro's shoulders in that scenario.

3. The "anti-Castro" Cuban exiles bait. Exiles, enraged that JFK did not provide air cover for the Bay of Pigs invasion, decide to kill him for revenge, as well as the hope that Johnson will then support them militarily.

Afterword

<u>Personnel</u>: Supposedly a team of anti-Castro exiles, so, if any Cuban exiles are caught, they can be characterized as mad for revenge, though not really part of the established anti-Castro movement.

4. The <u>"Mafia" bait.</u> Bobby Kennedy had been pursuing the Mob mercilessly, so his brother is killed to get Bobby off the mobsters' backs.

<u>Personnel</u>: Supposedly a couple of Mafia hit men, recruited from abroad so as not to be too easily tied to the Mob.

5. The <u>"Russian" bait.</u> A "defector" has been turned by the Russkies while in Russia, then sent back as a "sleeper," who is activated to kill JFK by the Russian assassin master Valery Kostikov in Mexico City. Same as the "lone nut" bait, but covered with caviar. Very dangerous bait, could start World War III, with atomic bombs.

<u>Personnel</u>: Supposedly 'Lee Harvey Oswald,' "defector" and "commie lover."

Since the plotters don't know which shooters or support personnel might be caught, they include some Mob people, some anti-Castro people, and, of course, the phony "lone nut" in the TSBD. The specific scenario to be promoted publicly will depend on circumstances and who is caught.

Note that all of these scenarios lead *away* from the CIA, except, of course, the CIA's involvement with the anti-Castro exiles. However, if a Mob plotter and an anti-Castro plotter are caught – well, everyone knows that the Mob and the anti-Castro people are working together to regain what they lost in Cuba.

The original concept was to make people think the assassination was carried out by a Cuban hit squad, whose act would launch a Cuban invasion, although it could lead to World War III. There must have been cross-currents in the upper echelons of the planners/supporters of the assassination, however, because somewhere along the line they decided not to risk a third world war with forty million Americans dead in one hour. So the cover story was shifted to the "lone nut," who would be killed by police, thus permanently closing the case.

Still, the "lone nut" scenario couldn't be promoted until 'Lee Harvey Oswald' was caught and killed 'resisting arrest,' hopefully within a couple of hours after JFK's death. The "lone nut" kept his killers at bay, however, so it took two days – but the "lone nut" *was* executed. The "lone nut" scenario has been promulgated for the past fifty plus years by the federal government and mainstream media, even though no intelligent person believes it after reading any one of the better books on the JFK assassination. Richard Nixon told one of his aides that it was the greatest hoax ever perpetrated. Richard Nixon! Please note: no one in the CIA, FBI, ONI, or Army Intelligence bit on any of the "hooks." They all knew this was a coup d'état.

So, who ordered the death of John Kennedy? JFK had done, was doing or planned to do the following:

1. had refused to provide U.S. air cover for the Bay of Pigs invasion of Cuba and refused other U.S. military support for the invasion,

2. had turned down proposed war plans directed against Castro's Cuba by both the CIA and the Pentagon,

3. had refused to consider a pre-emptive nuclear war against Russia, proposed by two generals,

4. had fired the top echelon of the CIA, and alienated top military officers,

5. had been in the process of getting rid of the Federal Reserve Bank – *a private enterprise*, owned by both U.S. and foreign bankers, which regulates U.S. currency and lends money to the U.S. government – by

having the U.S. Treasury put out its own currency ($4.2 billion in United States Notes was issued by the time of Kennedy's death), which would have eliminated the Federal Debt and the huge amounts of interest the U.S. was paying to the Federal Reserve (Note: U.S. Notes were discontinued in 1966 and the U.S. continues to be in debt – almost eighteen trillion dollars today, on which it pays interest),

6. had decided to get out of the Vietnam War, which would have:

a) avoided the need for the U.S. borrowing many billions of dollars from the Federal Reserve for the Vietnam War, from which the Fed would have received many billions in interest (and eventually did), and

b) deprived the Military Industrial Complex from reaping many billions in war profits (Note: Prez LBJ made sure all of his industrial friends – and his wife – made billions from the war),

7. had issued an Executive Order to begin pulling out U.S. troops from Vietnam – a thousand men a month, ending in 1965 (Note: LBJ *immediately* cancelled the pullout when he became president and eventually increased the number of troops there from

16,000 to 543,000 (2.6 million served in the war), with 58,000 U.S. deaths, 211,000 wounded, half a million with PTSD, over a million Vietnamese killed, with a cost of two trillion (in 2010 dollars), including veterans' benefits to date),

8. had been working with Khrushchev to end the Cold War and bring in an era of peace, which would have lost billions in war profits to the international bankers and the Military Industrial Complex,

9. had begun to break up the CIA (Note: LBJ let the CIA run rampant),

10. had begun to support the Civil Rights movement and enforce Civil Rights laws (Note: LBJ co-opted JFK's plans – already formulated – and made them seem like his own),

11. had planned to get rid of J. Edgar Hoover, who was reaching mandatory retirement age (Note: LBJ appointed his buddy Hoover FBI Director for life),

12. had planned to drop Lyndon Johnson from the 1964 Democratic ticket, after which LBJ would have been indicted for many crimes (Note: When Lyndon became president, all possible charges against him vanished),

13. intended to get rid of the oil depletion allowance, which would have cost the Texas oil barons many millions of dollars in profits (Note: LBJ kept the oil depletion allowance in place),

14. intended to wipe out the Mafia (Note: LBJ and Hoover immediately stopped pursuing the Mafia),

15. was expected to win the presidency again in a landslide vote (over 60%), with a good possibility that Robert Kennedy would run for president in 1968 after JFK's second term, which would have allowed the Kennedy brothers to reshape the United States economy and government, crippling the power of the Eastern "Establishment" and the giant corporations.

Who do you think gave the order to kill JFK? Follow the money trail and check out the boys who liked to play with power. Not hard to find them: you can see hundreds of names listed at the back of Richard Gilbride's book. There were others.

And let's get straight about who orchestrated the cover-up: Lyndon Johnson, FBI Director J. Edgar Hoover, former CIA Director Alan Dulles, Congressman Gerald Ford, and Chief Justice Earl Warren. The first three wanted to hide the truth, having been involved, at least in the coverup; then

Johnson convinced Warren that the 'truth' – that a Cuban hit squad shot JFK – could start an atomic war. Those five controlled the investigation and its report. Everyone else answered to them, right down the line.

Can you imagine that? Just one former and four then-current government "servants" basically raped the entire population of the United States of America! Compared to them, Benedict Arnold and John Wilkes Booth were very small potatoes. Commission members Louisiana Congressman Hale Boggs and Kentucky Senator John Sherman Cooper had doubts about the Warren Report, and Georgia Senator Richard Russell didn't want to sign off on it. Warren insisted they all had to.

And fifty-three years later the U.S. government is *still* hiding the truth! Why? All the conspirators have to be dead by now. But, of course, the present guardians of the gates would have to explain why *they've* been keeping the truth hidden, even to the present. It's sad, it's tragic, that so many were and are traitors to the people of the United States of America.

Doppelgänger: The Legend Of Lee Harvey Oswald

What Happened To:

Guy Banister. Died in June, 1964, age 63, of a 'heart attack,' before he could testify for the WC. All of his files were seized by government agents.

NOTE: In 1975 it was learned during the Church Committee hearings that the CIA had developed a poison which would cause a victim to have an immediate heart attack. The poison would be frozen into the shape of a dart and then fired from a pistol at such high speed that it would go through the clothes of the target, leaving just a tiny red mark. The poison would melt in the body, be absorbed into the blood stream and cause a heart attack. The drug was undetectable by modern autopsy procedures.

Dr. Mary Sherman. Died in July, 1964, age 51, suffered a terrible accident related to her cancer work.

Charles "Dutz" Murret. Died in 1964, age 63, "after a brief illness."

Earlene Roberts. Died in January, 1966, of a 'heart attack.' No autopsy was performed.

Jack Ruby. Died in January, 1967, age 55, of cancer – he said he had been injected with cancer cells; if so, they were likely the ones developed by Dr. Sherman. Ruby never revealed what he knew.

David Ferry. Died in February, 1967, age 48, of a brain hemorrhage, under questionable circumstances, as New Orleans D.A. Jim Garrison was about to call him to testify against Clay Shaw. The New Orleans coroner ruled his death "natural" – Jim Garrison believed it was murder.

J. Edgar Hoover. Died in May, 1972, age 77, of a 'heart attack.' May have been murdered by a fast-acting poison.

Lyndon Baines Johnson. Died in January, 1973, age 64, of a heart attack, an unhappy man.

Clay Shaw. Died oddly in August, 1974, age 61, and no autopsy was performed.

Roger Craig, Witness, former Dallas deputy sheriff. Died in May, 1975, age 39, after four attempts on his life over several years, the last attempt successful – shot to death.

George de Mohrenschildt. Died in March, 1977, age 65, *supposedly* a 'suicide' by shotgun, three hours after he was contacted by an investigator from the HSCA. The Sheriff's office called his death "very strange." No fingerprints were found on the weapon he *supposedly* used.

Billy Lovelady. Died in January, 1979, age 41, during the HSCA hearings, of a 'heart attack.'

'Marguerite Oswald.' Died in January, 1981, of cancer, real name and real age unknown. Had no contact with her 'sons' or 'daughter-in-law' after November, 1963.

Roy S. Truly. Died in November, 1985, age 78. He had been in fear for his life during the previous 22 years. Why?

James Jesus Angleton. Died in May, 1987, age 69, of lung cancer, telling his wife he had made a lot of mistakes.

David Atlee Phillips. Died in July, 1988, age 65, of cancer. Before his death, he told his brother James that he'd been in Dallas on November 22, 1963.

Richard Case Nagell. Died in October, 1995, age 65, of a 'heart attack' in Los Angeles. The day before his body was found, the ARRB had sent him a letter, having decided to pursue Nagell's private files and use the ARRB's subpoena power to call Nagell to testify. A footlocker full of documents he had preserved disappeared shortly after his death.

William Hoyt Shelley. Died in 1996, probably age 70, taking to the grave what he knew.

John Edward Pic. Died in April 2000, age 68, taking with him any secrets he possessed. In 1978, the Defense

Department acknowledged it had once investigated Pic, but it wouldn't reveal why.

E. Howard Hunt. Died in January, 2007, age 89, on his death bed revealing to a son names of some top conspirators.

Police Sergeant Jerry Hill. Died in July, 2011, age 81, keeping what he knew to himself.

James Files. Shooter. Still living, has been in prison for murder for many years.

Buell Wesley Frazier. Still living.

Ruth Hyde Paine. Still living.

Marina (Oswald) Porter. Still living. Remarried, had a son, Mark, with her second husband, Kenneth Porter. Oswald's daughters June and Rachel also are living.

Judyth Vary Baker. Still living. Had five children with her husband Robert, then they divorced, in 1987. Judyth wrote two books in recent years, about 'Lee' and David Ferrie, now lives somewhere in Europe following death threats.

Robert L. Oswald. Still living. In 1997 researcher John Armstrong noted that "neither June nor Rachel [Oswald] have ever met, spoken to, or received correspondence from Robert Oswald: as of 1997, no communication whatsoever from their 'Uncle Robert.'"

Author's Note

It is long past the time for some basic facts to be nailed down, and these can be acquired, if the will is there. Suggestions:

1. DNA samples should be requested from the children of Harvey Oswald, Robert Oswald, and John Pic, to determine if Harvey's children have the DNA of the Oswald/Claverie/Pic family. If not, then we will know there were indeed two Lee Harvey Oswalds. DNA analysis would also reveal what part of the world Harvey Oswald came from.

2. The president should do four simple things:

   a. Rescind President Johnson's executive order to keep the assassination records sealed for 75 years and order all records unsealed now.

   b. Order the release of all federal income tax records of "Lee Harvey Oswald" and "Marguerite Oswald," *both* sets of those individuals, also "Harvey Lee Oswald" and "Marguerite Claverie Oswald."

c. Order the CIA, FBI, ONI, Army Intelligence, and INS to disclose the real name and background of the "Lee Harvey Oswald" (Harvey Lee Oswald) killed by Jack Ruby, and the real name and background of "Marguerite Oswald," 'Oswald's mother', with no phony talk of "national security," relating to this information. Also "Alck James Hidell," and all variations of that name, such as "Alex," including initials, used by Harvey Oswald.

These actions should reveal who "Lee Harvey Oswald" and "Marguerite Oswald" really were and throw needed light on the JFK conspiracy.

Acknowledgement

This book could not have been written without the dedicated research and writing of thousands of citizen investigators over the past fifty plus years, especially the monumental research of John Armstrong. Some of their names and publications are listed below.

Many brave witnesses, many killed, must also be acknowledged.

Doppelgänger: The Legend Of Lee Harvey Oswald

Sources

Books

Armstrong, John. *Harvey And Lee: How The CIA Framed Oswald*. 2003.

Baker, Judyth Vary. *Me & Lee*. 2011.

_____. *David Ferrie*. 2014.

Belzer, Richard and Wayne, David. *Hit List*. 2013.

Benson, Michael. *Who's Who In The JFK Assassination*. 1993, 2003.

Bishop, Jim. *The Day Kennedy Was Shot*. 1968.

Davis, John H. *Mafia Kingfish*. 1989.

DiEugenio, James (ed.) and Pease, Lisa (ed.). *The Assassinations*. 2003.

Douglas, James W. *JFK And The Unspeakable*. 2010.

Ernest, Barry. *The Girl On The Stairs*. 2013.

Fetzer, James H. *Murder In Dealey Plaza*. 2000.

Fonzi, Gaeton. *The Last Investigation*. 2013.

Garrison, Jim. *On The Trail Of The Assassins*. 1991.

Gilbride, Richard. *Matrix For Assassination*. 2009.

Gillon, S. M. *Lee Harvey Oswald: 48 Hours To Live*. 2013.

Groden, R. J. *The Search For Lee Harvey Oswald*. 1995.

Groden, R. J. and Livingstone, H. E. *High Treason*. 1989.

Harris, Patrick. *See No Evil*. 2014.

Haslam, Edward T. *Dr. Mary's Monkey*. 2014.

Hepburn, James and Turner, William. *Farewell America: The Plot To Kill JFK*. 2002.

Janney, Peter. *Mary's Mosaic*. 2013.

Kantor, Seth. *The Ruby Coverup*. 1980.

Krusch, Barry. *Impossible: The Case Against Lee Harvey Oswald (Volume Two)*. 2012.

Lane, Mark. *Plausible Denial*. 1991.

Livingstone, Harrison Edward. *High Treason 2*. 1992.

Marrs, Jim. *Crossfire: The Plot That Killed Kennedy*. 2013.

McBride, Joseph. *Into The Nightmare*. 2013.

Meagher, Sylvia. *Subject Index To The Warren Report and Hearings & Exhibits*. 1966.

_____. *Accessories After The Fact*. 1967, 2013.

Melanson, Philip H. *Spy Saga: Lee Harvey Oswald And U.S. Intelligence*. 1990.

Morley, Jefferson. *Our Man In Mexico*. 2008.

Newman, John. *Oswald And The CIA*. 2008.

Oliver, B., w/ Buchanan, C. *Nightmare In Dallas*. 1994.

Oswald, Robert L. *Lee*. 1967.

O'Toole, George. *The Assassination Tapes*. 1975.

Palamara, Vincent Michael. *Survivor's Guilt*. 2013.

Roberts, Craig. *Kill Zone*. 2014.

Roberts, Craig, with Armstrong, John. *JFK: The Dead Witnesses*. 2014.

Russell, Dick. *The Man Who Knew Too Much*. 1992.

_____. *On The Trail Of The JFK Assassins*. 2008.

Scott, Peter Dale. *Deep Politics.* 1996.

Smith, Matthew. *JFK: The Second Plot*. 2002.

_____. *Say Goodbye To America*. 2005.

Stone, Roger, with Colapietro, Mike. *The Man Who Killed Kennedy*. 2013.

Summers, Anthony. *Conspiracy*. 1980.

Twyman, Noel H. *Bloody Treason: The Assassination Of John F. Kennedy*. 2010.

Warren Commission. Testimonies & Exhibits. 1964.

Weberman, Alan J. and Canfield, Michael. *Coup d'Etat In America*. 1992.

Weisberg, Harold. *Whitewash*. 2013.

_____. *Whitewash II*. 2013.

_____. *Whitewash III*. 2013.

Internet

Abrams, Malcolm. *JFK Murder Hatched In Ruby Club*.

Altgens, James. *Altgens6 Photograph*.

Armstrong, John. *Comrade Harvey & Agent Lee*.

_____. *Harvey And Lee.*

_____. *Harvey & Lee: How The CIA Framed Oswald.*

_____. *Harvey & Lee Home Page.*

_____. *Harvey, Lee And Tippit.*

_____. *Jack Ruby.*

_____. *Just The Facts Please.*

_____. *Manipulated, Fabricated, Disappearing Evidence.*

_____. *Marines To Minsk.*

_____. *November In Dallas: 1997 Presentation "Harvey & Lee."*

_____. *November 22, 1963.*

_____. *Oswald Did Not Purchase A Pistol From Seaport Traders.*

_____. *Oswald Did Not Purchase A Rifle From Klein's.*

_____. *The Early Lives Of Harvey And Lee.*

_____. *The Pre-Arranged Murder Of Officer Tippit.*

_____. *University Of Minnesota Speech.*

Assassination Research. *November 22, 1963.*

Bailey, George W. *Allen Dulles And The Doppelgängers.*

_____. *Lee H. Oswald's Name Missing From SSDI.*

Sources

Benson, R. *JFK, Oswald, And The Raleigh Connection*.

Biffle, Kent. *This Couldn't Be Happening*.

Bisaro, Anna. *Oswald Got 'Very, Very Lucky.'*

Brussell, Mae. *The Last Words Of Lee Harvey Oswald*.

Cinque, Ralph, with Fetzer, Jim. *JFK: 49 Years In The Offing — The Altgens Reenactment*.

Cochran, Mike. *I Was A Pallbearer...*.

Craig, John S. *The Guns Of Dealey Plaza*.

Craig, Roger. *When They Kill A President*.

D. C. Police Department. *Mauser*.

Drenas, Bill. *An Overlooked Texas Theatre Witness*.

_____. Car #10 Where Are You?

_____. *The Top Ten Record Shop*.

Ericson, Greg. *48th JFK Anniversary*.

FBI Report. *Evelyn Harris*.

Fetzer, James H., with Baker, Judyth Vary. *JFK: Judyth Vary Baker Cements Oswald In The Doorway*.

Files, James E. *Confession Of James E. Files.*

Fleming, Trish and Jendro, Zach. *The Curious Case Of The American Bakeries Pay Voucher*.

Fritz, J. W. *Report Of Interrogation Of Lee Harvey Oswald*.

George, M. Waldo. *Affidavit*.

Gilbride, Richard. *William Shelley – Betrayal And Perjury*.

Golz, Earl. *Was Oswald In Window?*

Hewett, Carol. *Silencers, Sniper Rifles, & The CIA.*

History Matters. *Oswald, The CIA, And Mexico City.*

_____. *Jack Hammond, CE 3001.*

Hooke, Richard, with Fetzer, Jim. *Oswald Wasn't Even A Shooter.*

_____. *Bill Shelley's Shrunken Head.*

Hopsicker, Daniel. *Barry Seal, The CIA Camp In Lacombe....*

Jfk1963. *Acme Building Maintenance.*

JFKCalc. *Dealey Plaza: Witness Surveys.*

JFK Facts. *Greg Parker.*

JFK Lancer. *Ruth And Michael Paine.*

Jones, Penn, Jr. *Forgive My Grief II.*

_____. *Forgive My Grief: v. 1-4.*

Mary Ferrell Foundation.

Myers, Dale K. *Oswald's Mail-Order Revolver Purchase.*

Morrow, Robert. *The LBJ-CIA Assassination Of JFK.*

National Archives and Records Admin. *William Shelley.*

Oswald Innocence Campaign. *The Likeness Of Oswald And Doorman.*

Parker, Greg. *Neely Street Questions, Page 2.*

Palamara, Vince. *On Security And Secret Service.*

Parnell, W. Tracy. *The Exhumation Of Lee Harvey Oswald.*

Sources

Plumlee, Robert "Tosh." *Declaration*.

Proctor, Grover B., Jr. *The Raleigh Call*.

Prouty, Fletcher. *The Guns Of Dallas*.

Reitzes, David. *Constructing The Assassin, Part 4*.

Reopen Kennedy Case. *Jack Edwin Dougherty*.

Rivera, Larry, with Fetzer, Jim. *JFK: Why Buell Wesley Frazier Was Erased From Altgens6*.

Rivera, Larry, and Schaeffer, Roy: *The James "Ike" Altgens JFK Photo Timeline.*

Roberts, Earlene. *Affidavit*.

Russell, Dick. *Oswald And The CIA*.

Schmidt, Markus. *Pierce M. Allman*.

_____. *Buell Wesley Frazier*.

Texas State Library Archives, Attorney General's Office.

The National Archives Catalog. *George, M. Waldo*.

United States Federal Census, 1940. *Emil Kardos*.

Warren Commission. *Guide To Numbered Exhibits*.

Warren Commission. *List Of Exhibits*.

_____. *JFK Assassination Witness Page*.

_____. *CE 1381*.

_____. *Exhibit 150.*

_____. *Exhibit 162.*

_____. *Exhibit 369.*

Doppelgänger: The Legend Of Lee Harvey Oswald

_____. *Exhibit 369- detail*.

_____. *Exhibit 440*.

_____. *Exhibit 1061*.

_____. *Exhibit 1118*.

_____. *Exhibit 1150*.

Wernerhoff, Carl. *The Neely Street Mysteries*.

WDSU. *Transcript Of FPCC Debate*.

Weston, William. *The Spider's Web: The Texas School Book Depository And The Dallas Conspiracy*.

_____. *The Glaze Letters*.

_____. *411 Elm Street*.

Wikipedia. *Voice Stress Analysis*.

Wilcott, James. *Testimony*.

Yusuf, Gokay Hasan. *Gerald Hill And The Murder Of Officer Tippit - Part 1*.

_____. *Gerald Hill And The Murder Of Officer Tippit – Part 2*.

_____. *Gerald Hill And The Framing Of Lee Harvey Oswald*.

DVD

Dankbaar, Wim. *Confessions From The Grassy Knoll*.

Newspapers

New York Herald Tribune, November 23, 1963.

The Dallas Morning News, November 23, 1963.

Author

George Schwimmer, Ph.D., was a theatre director for thirty years, as well as teaching theatre at two colleges and a university. He later studied film at UCLA Extension, and was VP of Development for a Los Angeles TV film producer. He currently writes books, screenplays and plays, including HAMLET DEAD and CAYCE. To reach him: www.GeorgeSchwimmer.com. NOTE: There also is a Kindle eBook version of this book, with some of the photographs in color.

Made in the USA
San Bernardino, CA
24 September 2016